DR. JESSICA METCALFE

Speak Kindly, You're Listening
Copyright © 2022 by Dr. Jessica E. Metcalfe
Cover photograph by Adam and Kev Photography

All rights reserved. No part of this publication may be reproduced, distributed, or transmitted in any form or by any means, including photocopying, recording or other electronic or mechanical methods, without the prior written permission of the author, except in the case of brief quotations embodied in reviews and certain other non-commercial uses permitted by copyright law.

Printed in the United States of America
Hardcover ISBN: 978-1-958714-41-6
Paperback ISBN: 978-1-958714-42-3
Ebook ISBN: 978-1-958714-43-0
Library of Congress Control Number: 2022949011

This book was written from my perspective. The memories that I am sharing (that include family and friends) may, in your mind, be reflected differently; but, this is what I saw, felt and experienced.

CHICAGO·NEWYORK·PARIS·ROME

Muse Literary
3319 N. Cicero Avenue
Chicago IL 60641-9998

For additional information please visit
https://www.drjessicametcalfe.com/home

Valerie,
Let that inner cheerleader
shine through.

ADVANCE PRAISE FOR *SPEAK KINDLY, YOU'RE LISTENING*

"It's a beautiful piece of work. You can hear Jessica's raw, emotional and powerful voice the entire way through."
—Dr. Keely Matheson, dentist, clinic owner

"Infused with great insight and knowledge, an inspiration for all high-performers navigating their inner gremlin."
—Frank King, The Mental Health Comedian and 7 Time TEDx Talker

"Dr. Jessica has written an engaging and interactive read that feels like one 'ah-hah' moment after another. It left me feeling inspired and wanting to take action on conquering my own inner gremlin."
—Megan Wheeler, chief of staff, Level Access

"Every woman will benefit from reading this book. Dr. Metcalfe breaks down how and why we make ourselves miserable, how it's holding us back, and provides the tangible tools we need to step into the life and mindset we've been working so hard to achieve."
—Dr. P. Robus

"Dr. Jessica Metcalfe's *Speak Kindly, You're Listening* is a treasure trove of wisdom, encouragement and solid guidance. The next must read in personal growth - it will help anyone wanting to improve their career and life! Fans of Brene Brown will love!"
—Sara Connell, #1 bestselling author of *The Science of Getting Rich for Women*

"Dr. Metcalfe connects the dots between personal development and psychology with her vivid personal experiences and science-based methods to break the cycles of Imposter Phenomenon, Perfectionism, and Burnout. It is both empowering and practical, and extremely personally relevant as a woman in dentistry and entrepreneurship; I felt as though she was speaking directly to me!"
—Shivani Kamodia Barto, DDS, yoga teacher, wellness coach, and founder of Dr.ShivAsana

To Keely and Alero, you are both the sisters I never had and the family I choose. Thank you for being my cheerleaders when I could only hear my gremlin.

To Esme, I will be your cheerleader when you are only starting to learn what your inner voice is saying.

TABLE OF CONTENTS

TO FEEL

I feel as deep as the ocean depths are dark.
I feel as great as flames separate and part.
I feel as sturdy as the mountains are high.
I feel as powerful as the winds blow by.

I used to think that my feelings were wrong.
I used to think that my feelings were oh too strong.
I used to think that my feelings were bad.
I used to think that my feelings were oh too grand.

Can the ocean be too deep?
Can the fire be too weak?
Can the earth be too meek?
Can the air be too unique?

My answer, no.
Instead, I grow.

I now know that my feelings are not wrong.
In fact, my emotions are right and strong.

This, is why
I feel excitement in my toes.
This, is why
I feel sadness to my bones.

My feelings are my journey to be learned.
My feelings are my experience in this world.
—Dr. Jessica E. Metcalfe

INTRODUCTION

When I was in my deepest, darkest abyss, I kept hearing myself ask the same questions over and over: "Why as a high-achieving woman do I feel the need to continuously prove my worth to everyone? Why do I feel empty, alone, and not enough? Why am I unable to ask for help? And why do I feel the pressure to be perfect?" If I combined all of these questions, what it really came down to was: **"Why as high-achieving women do we experience what we experience?"**

I initially set out on this journey in hopes of finding answers and healing for myself. In doing so, I stumbled into more and more literature about what high-achieving women had to say. Then I realized I wasn't the only one experiencing this. In fact, others felt the same; they felt alone, and yet no one talked about the shame, frustration, resentment, and anger that come from being a high-achieving woman.

So I started writing a book a few years ago, around 2018. Actually, I started two other books in the last five years. Every time I sat down to write, it didn't feel right. It wasn't until the fall of 2021 when I realized I was writing the wrong books. Maybe those books will come back into fruition in the future, but this book you are reading right now was a labor of love and pain. Writing this book helped me heal my own wounds and showed me how far I have come and how the future holds so many adventures for me to explore. I say adventures because that's exactly what they are: adventures that come with ups and downs, good times and bad times, but adventures nonetheless.

As a kid, you may have heard the saying, "Stick and stones may break my bones, but words can never hurt me." That is a total lie. Words are powerful and have meaning. In fact, the way you choose to speak to yourself has a direct impact on your mental, physical, emotional, and spiritual self.

My deep, dark abyss scared the crap out of me.

I thought: "This is it. This is life. This is what I deserve."

But what I didn't realize was that this is what I had *convinced* myself I deserved. My inner voice, my inner critic, had spoken to me negatively for so long, I knew no different. **There was no inner cheerleader because I didn't allow her to exist.**

Then one day, when I was a couple of years into my healing journey, I finally woke up and said, "I'm tired of always being scared."

For years I was scared of making a mistake. I was scared of making the wrong decision. I was scared of what others would think. I was scared I wouldn't fit in. I was scared I'd say the wrong thing or piss someone off. I was scared I would never be good enough. And finally, after years, I didn't want to be scared anymore.

On paper, my life looked great. In 2017 I was a new general dentist, having just completed a hospital residency program treating special needs and medically compromised patients. I had been sought out to become a staff dentist at a world-renowned cancer centre, eventually becoming education director, special project manager, and, for a short period of time, acting deputy chief of dentistry. I was involved in organized dentistry from the local to provincial associations and sat on national education committees, while also being an instructor at a dental school. I also worked another job as an associate dentist and was on the precipice of owning my own office. It all looked good on paper because I was stepping out of my comfort zone; but on the inside, I was dying in a pit of darkness and despair that terrified me. That darkness was where my inner gremlin lived and haunted me on a daily basis. I accomplished all these achievements because that is what I had conditioned myself to do: become a high achiever at all costs in the name of being "successful and happy." But I felt neither of them.

Around this time, I started speaking at hospital and dental conferences about treating cancer patients from my point of view as a dentist. I noticed a gap in the dental curriculum. There were lectures on "how to diagnose head and neck cancer," but there were no conversations about treating patients post–cancer therapy and how dentists can improve a patient's quality of life. This is where my passion lies: asking questions and listening to patients' needs, wants, and concerns, and putting together a personalized action plan to improve their quality of life.

For the five years I was at the cancer centre, I made it a priority to sit and listen to my patients and help them navigate their challenges and concerns post–cancer therapy. On numerous occasions, my patients continued to see me long after their treatment was complete. They often said, "You just have this energy, and I like coming to see you." I didn't really understand this, because I had also been told on separate occasions that I can be too loud and intense.

A few years passed and what I noticed anecdotally (later confirmed through research), was that patients with a positive mindset do better pre-, during, and post-therapy. Yes, being diagnosed with cancer sucks, but the person who recognizes it for what it is and then fights, day in and day out, comes out the other side with fewer side effects and faster healing. This is called informed optimism, which I go into later in this book. It's not about being positive every day, but embracing the shittiness that allows you to get to the other side. This experience comes with heavy tears and deep laughs. Both are needed.

The question you are probably asking yourself is: "How do cancer patients connect to high-achieving women?" Well, treating cancer patients opened my eyes to the human's mental strength and resilience. I am honored to have been a part of so many lives, however long or short our time together. That's when it came to me: if I could teach how to improve a patient's quality of life post–cancer therapy, then teaching dentists to improve their own quality of life could be a natural transition. I was tired of hearing of how high the depression, anxiety and suicide rates were and still are today. So I got my life coaching certificate, dove into psychology research and textbooks and started running programs. Then, a trend popped up: the individuals reaching out to me were mainly women; high-achieving women across all different careers. That's how I went from teaching dentists how to improve patients' quality of life to coaching and speaking to high-achieving women. In this book, I am sharing my story, my clients' stories, and the literature I've gathered to help high-achieving women improve their quality of life.

Teaching comes naturally to me. When I was fourteen, I started teaching piano at the Royal Ontario Conservatory of Music, eventually starting my own rock 'n' music school at age eighteen. Thus, it was a no-brainer for me to found The Alchemist Dentist in 2019 and then rebrand into Alchemy Academy the summer of 2022 due to expansion outside of dentistry. My mission is to create safe spaces for high-achieving women to step into their vulnerability so they can recognize their true potential by changing their inner narrative. I've coached dozens of women (and men) and companies on the importance of mental well-being by understanding how one chooses to speak to oneself. Alchemy Academy has values that include: creating progress over perfection, choosing weirdness over fitting in, being open-minded to learn and grow, debating kindly and with friendly communication, allowing magic and science to work together, building collaboration instead of competition, and believing confidence is queen!

Throughout this book I have used pronouns and vocabulary like *she, her, queen,* and *woman.* But, this book is for any high achiever. Period. These tips and research apply to the high achievers who have an inner voice that speaks unkindly to themselves, however they choose to identify.

My work at Alchemy Academy combines all I've learned from my time with cancer patients, the literature I dove headfirst into, my teaching style (compared to old ways of fear-based learning), and my coaching certificate. I have created programs and workshops for my clients and for companies to make changes they didn't realize were possible. All of these things bring me back to this book: I want you to know that making changes for yourself is totally possible, **and it all starts with how you choose to speak to yourself.**

This book is a condensed version of what I teach and speak on, and it is broken down into four parts: 1. Impostor Phenomenon, 2. Perfectionism, 3. Burnout, and 4. Darkness. Within each part, I have incorporated my story, my clients' stories, and the research I have found relevant to each section. I want to thank all of my clients for allowing me to be with you on your journey of development. Names of clients and patients in the book have been changed to provide anonymity.

To date, I have been a guest on numerous podcasts including *Best Boss Ever*, and I have given keynote speeches and lectures to WNORTH, Key Media, Women in Wealth Management, Women Entrepreneurs, and multiple national dental organizations. In the winter of 2022, I started my own podcast called *The Dark Side of Dentistry: The Shit No One Talks About*, where guests share their stories about how they've navigated through their inner critic. As of recently, the podcast has been rebranded to *Speak Kindly, You're Listening*, where guests from all areas of work and life can share their stories.

Here's how I suggest you read the book: go in with an open mind instead of getting angry at yourself for doing it "wrong." Use your experiences and learn from them, because if you are currently struggling, know that you don't have to keep struggling.

Throughout the book, I have provided many real-life examples as well as opportunities for you to explore a different way of doing things in real time.

You will also find what I like to call "brain training exercises," which help you start your journey of doing the internal work. Mental fitness is just as important as physical fitness. Though mental fitness isn't as visual, you will still notice physical, mental, emotional, and spiritual changes. If you get discouraged at any point along the way, I want you to remind yourself that it is totally normal and all a part of progress. Without challenges, we can't realize our truest potential. An additional bonus for you is that you get VIP access to my online book portal, which has a wealth of extra brain training exercises with videos. Head over to www.speakkindlyyourelistening.com for these additional resources.

Nowadays, I only practice clinical dentistry one to two days a week, and eventually I will be phasing it out altogether because my joy is in helping women change their inner narrative. I love being able to empower women, not just to fill their resume and show me what they are good at, but to see them step into their own power, strength, and confidence in being a woman . . . a *badass goddess warrior.*

What I hope you get from the book is a sense of community and belonging, knowing you are not alone in your experiences of navigating challenges and painful emotions; that you will know your inner voice can be full of strength, power, and confidence, and that you can own it. Gone are the days of belittling yourself or feeling ashamed of who you are. It is time to step out of your inner critic's shadow and into the limelight, where I give you permission to hold space. It's time for you to give yourself permission, too. Here we go!

PART I
IMPOSTOR PHENOMENON

"I am not who you think I am;
I am not who I think I am;
I am who I think you think I am."
—Charles Horton Cooley, American sociologist

CHAPTER 1

WHAT IS IMPOSTOR PHENOMENON?

I stood in the operating room (OR), staring at the nurse, hesitant about what I should do next. The anesthetized patient lay on the operating table in front of me, oxygen tubes hanging from the mouth. I was a hospital dental resident treating medically compromised and special needs patients and was only a few days into the start of my residency program. The program director stepped out of the OR twenty minutes earlier because he thought I would take longer, but I was already finished with the procedures on one side of the mouth.

When dentists take a patient to the OR, the preferred placement of intubation for oxygen is through the nose. That way we have access to our operatory field, the mouth. In this case, we placed the intubation by mouth because the patient's nose anatomy didn't allow for it.

Only having graduated dental school two months earlier, I now stood in the operating room with a nurse and the anesthesiologist, and I was second in command from the program director himself. This wasn't my first time in the OR, but it was the first time I completed all clinical procedures on my own including x-rays, deep cleaning, fillings, and any necessary extractions. It was a lot of dentistry all at once. These patients had a developmental delay or musculoskeletal spasms where dentistry in a usual clinic setting would be unsafe.

I was confident in my skills, and I believed in who I was as a dental clinician. In this moment, the nurse and I continued to stare at each other. A few minutes passed and I stood motionless, waiting, because I was told not to switch the intubation sides until the program director returned.

Because we had to intubate by mouth for this patient, the tubing itself draped along one side of the mouth, blocking complete access and vision to do dentistry on that side. When we intubate through the mouth, we also need to place coverage at the back of the throat so our dental materials or fluids like water and blood don't travel into the patient's lungs.

Thus, changing the intubation sides can be a cumbersome process for the patient, the nurse, the doctor, and the anesthesiology team. Switching the intubation sides can take anywhere from five to fifteen minutes.

Now that I was waiting, not doing any dentistry, I was wasting OR time. I had to make a decision: continue to wait until he came back, or switch intubation sides. I took a deep breath and turned to the nurse and the anesthesiologist, "Let's switch sides."

Both paused, looked at each other, and nodded their heads in agreement. As a team, the three of us moved the intubation tube, assessed the monitors, clamped the tubing for security, placed a throat pack to protect the lungs, and reevaluated the patient's general stability. It all went as planned.

I was well into the next procedure when the OR door flew open. The program director stomped in, and instantly, I could feel his stare on the back of my head.

"What did you do? Hands off and step away from my patient," he snarled.

I slowly put down the drill and the tiny mirror, raised my hands, and took a step backwards from the patient. The nurse and anesthesiologist looked at me with remorseful eyes; they were apologizing. My program director had a reputation of verbally, emotionally, and mentally abusing his residents. He even went as far as kicking residents out of the OR and out of his program. To me, this wasn't teaching nor mentoring. This was a form of humiliation and fear-based learning. I didn't know what I was getting into when I signed up for this program.

In a familiar hostile and furious tone, he said, "I told you not to change sides. I told you I needed to approve the other side before you moved on. I don't trust you with *my* patients."

He slowly approached me and the patient. It sounded like the patient's heart monitor sped up, but it wasn't the patient's. It was the thundering of my own heartbeat in my ears. Sweat dripped down my back, my glasses started to fog, and I could swear the nurse gasped. With each step he took, I started to question my abilities. *Did I do a good job? Did I finish the procedures? Did I do the right thing?*

Now standing next to me, leaning forward and looking at the patient, he growled, "I can't visualize the field because of the tubing; we won't be able to assess until this side is done. Get on with it."

I stepped back toward the patient and picked up my instruments, feeling the anger steaming from him and knowing that every single movement was now being watched meticulously. Any wrong step, any wrong glance, anything I did that wasn't a part of "his" way of doing things, I knew I would be reprimanded. In that moment, I felt scared and inadequate. I thought anything I did wasn't going to be the right thing for him.

Why was the hostile and furious tone so familiar? Because it hurtled me right back to my childhood and early adult years and how my father acted toward me. It didn't matter what I did right because he could only see the wrong. I got good grades for the most part, played sports, helped out at home, didn't do drugs, followed house "orders," and yet, when I left clothes on my bedroom floor, I was grounded. If anything, and I mean *anything* was out of sorts, my dad yelled at me. Over time, I created a mental shield to protect myself. To this day, I still can't remember exactly what he would say.

However, there are still moments I experience a deep feeling of worthlessness when someone gets angry and yells at me for doing something wrong according to their rules. It doesn't happen often, but that initial hardwiring has taken years to rewire and reframe.

One of the last arguments I remember having with my father was Easter weekend 2010, when I was twenty-two years old. It was the tipping point of how I saw myself in this family and who I was as an adult. I had come home, albeit against my wishes. I wanted to stay on school campus to finish my thesis, but I came home to appease my parents. I hated going home because I was the punching bag, verbally, mentally, and emotionally. I set myself up in the dining room so I could write my thesis, leaving papers and my computer sprawled across the table. I was in my creative flow.

At some point that weekend, my parents argued. That argument didn't remain with them, it overflowed into my life. My memory is hazy when it comes to specifics, but there likely was yelling, name-calling, belittling, door slamming, and a broken object. What haunts me is a vivid memory of walking back to the dining room after I received the brunt end of the fight. I sat down, opened my laptop, and began typing as tears dripped down my face. I didn't want to tolerate this hostility anymore. This isn't how I wanted to live.

As I silently cried, a little voice crept into my head and whispered, "*You will never be enough.*" I'm not sure what brought upon the thought. It could have been because of what my dad had just said to me, or because of how long it was taking me to write my thesis, or because I still hadn't been accepted into dental school.

The combined voices of others along with my own would become the dark voice I heard all the time, *my inner critic.* Little did I know, the way I chose to speak to myself would lead to my mental and emotional demise, my darkness.

I thought I was broken. I questioned everything. I felt like I couldn't do anything right. This resounding voice played over and over in my head, saying, "*You know you can't do this, you know someone else should be doing this, you know you're not capable . . . are you even worth it?*"

My inner critic was the only voice I heard. Every day for years, it's all I believed. No matter what people said to me, whether it was good or bad, it didn't matter. It was as if a record was on repeat and the record player wouldn't stop. I couldn't escape that voice. The voice was a whisper, and yet it sounded like screams, especially in moments of silence. *No matter what you do, you know you'll never be good enough.*

Back in the OR, I stood shaking in fear as I completed the last procedure. The program director sensed my fear because I could only see the smirk in his eyes, taunting me. He knew the power he had over me as a resident. As I finished the final procedure, I informed the anesthesiologist we were ready to check the other side. I could feel a bead of sweat slowly leave my hamstring toward the space behind my knee. The sweat hit my calf and felt like a hundred-pound weight. *What if I made a mistake? What if I have to redo a procedure? What if I missed something?* I took a deep breath.

He examined the patient's mouth, looked up, peered over his face mask, and warned, "You're lucky."

This was his approval. I could see the nurse and anesthesiologist let out the breath they likely didn't know they were holding.

I stood there repeating those words in my head. *You're lucky. You're lucky.* I knew this year was going to bring its challenges. But I didn't know this was going to be the year I started to walk into a deep, dark abyss, not knowing if I could find my way out.

Every day during this time, I woke up and chose to speak unkindly to myself. My voice was a blade and my confidence the shield that was cut into pieces. With my blade drawn, I found parts of me that were already wounded and applied pressure, reminding myself: *You're not good enough. You're not pretty enough. You're not skinny enough.* The blade entered the wound and cut deeper, turning to my personal qualities. *Your laugh is ugly. You're too loud and boisterous. You're stupid. You're too much.* Followed by the final twist. *This is why you are single. This is why you won't be a good leader. This is why you'll never find love. This is why you can't . . .*

I had convinced myself the voice was normal. Without me knowing, my inner critic shredded my confidence. Day by day, year by year, bit by bit, my confidence was cut into tiny little pieces and scattered across my conscious and unconscious mind. That voice crippled me and kept me stuck. That voice was my own worst enemy, hiding in plain sight.

But didn't everyone speak to themselves like this? Didn't other women doubt their own abilities? Didn't other women pick apart their flaws? I relied on that voice to motivate me, to allow me to set high standards and expectations. It allowed me to strive for perfection. It made me work hard—harder than I had ever done in my entire life. Most of all, I would scoff at people who thought highly of themselves.

That inner critic had convinced me it kept me humble. I did indeed smile at times, thanking myself for being modest. But my version of being modest and humble meant I underestimated my abilities, explained away my successes, always said "yes" (even when I wanted to say "no"), and discounted all my hard work. Hearing *you're lucky* was confirmation I didn't work hard enough, that I didn't have the skills or knowledge, that I wasn't good enough. If I was lucky, then that luck would eventually run out. I wouldn't be able hold up the façade any longer. Eventually, someone was going to figure it out: that I didn't belong, that I was a fraud.

Let me introduce you to *Impostor Phenomenon.* You may have heard the term impostor syndrome, but let's get something straight right from the beginning. It isn't a syndrome. There is nothing wrong with you. This isn't a diagnosis, and you are not broken. **Impostor Phenomenon (IP) is just that, a phenomenon, an event and feeling experienced by an exceptional person.** And that is you, the reader. You are the high achiever, high performer, all-around powerful woman. You may be a parent (to kids or pets), a caregiver, an athlete, an intellectual, a professional, and many more titles. YOU are exceptional beyond measure, and I am here to remind you of that. Together, you and I will build your confidence, change your inner narrative, and believe in your abilities.

Impostor Phenomenon is that intense feeling of internalized fear where you doubt your skills, talents, and accomplishments. You think you will be found out or exposed as a fraud. It's not that you think you have never accomplished something. It's that you don't believe it. It can occur with challenges or obstacles, trying something new, or if you are in a transitional period in your life (promotions, job change, becoming a parent, or moving).[1 2 3]

When I stood in the OR and made the decision to switch intubation sides, I trusted in my knowledge and abilities. If not, I would have continued to stand there aimlessly. Some part of me (and some part of you) knows you have the skills and abilities to do what you dream of doing. But, when you hear comments like *you're lucky,* it gives proof to your inner critic that your confidence should stay hidden. Your inner critic is playing a game of hide-and-seek with your confidence. While your confidence runs and hides, your inner critic is counting back from ten but never reaches one. This can all be going on in the background without you even knowing.

CHAPTER 2

BIRTH OF THE INNER CRITIC

A couple of years ago, I interviewed eighteen successful men and women across the dental, medical, and business industries. I asked the same five questions but my favourite question was, "Is self-doubt bad?" Each one of them had some version of the same answer, "Self-doubt isn't bad until it is." Self-doubt is not IP, and there is a large difference. Doubt encompasses a feeling of uncertainty in yourself. IP uses your doubt to convince yourself that you're a fraud, stifling your growth.

Self-doubt can be good because it keeps you on your toes, pushes you outside your comfort zone, and reminds you that you, in fact, care. Self-doubt is a part of your growth and evolution as a woman and a human being. When self-doubt keeps you stuck, your inner critic confirms all the nasty things you keep saying to yourself. Your inner critic uses this information as if it's ironclad so you question your abilities. This is how the inner critic pokes holes in your confidence.

This is the myth we keep telling ourselves, over and over again. The myth is a mind-trap known as *cognitive dissonance,* which incites a constant battle in our mind of expectations we set for ourselves and how we choose to view them. There is no winner on this battlefield, but there are a lot of wounds. Over time, the wounds become deep and trapped in our subconscious.

The IP belief origin can be broken down into two parts: (1) upbringing and (2) social conditioning or societal expectations.

UPBRINGING

This is not a blame game. I share this knowledge so you can figure out how that inner voice came to be. I repeat, this is not a blame game on what our parents or family passed on to us. If intelligence was highly valued growing up as a kid, this could have contributed to feelings of IP. Parents, caregivers, or other family members may have put an enormous amount of pressure and stress on being perfect, which was then followed by some sort of praise. Do well, get a ribbon. Get straight As, parents acknowledge you. You may have even seen your siblings or cousins be reprimanded for not getting high grades or winning competitions (like sports or music). Being perfect, being the best, and reaching those high expectations may have been ingrained in you from the get-go. Give yourself some ease when you ask yourself, *Why do I keep pushing myself past my limits?*

On the other side of the coin, you may have had a traumatic childhood. That could include verbal, emotional or physical abuse, a traumatic experience, or parents with mental illness. Having been exposed to this early on during your developmental and impressionable years, this can contribute to wanting to avoid your history and pushing yourself beyond measurable expectations. Childhood traumas can affect you long after the trauma is over, leaving you feeling empty, alone, vulnerable, and fragile, thinking you're never enough. This can be carried into adulthood.

I'm going to be honest. Raising kids is hard. When I worked through (and continue to work through) childhood trauma, I have to keep reminding myself my parents did the best they could with the knowledge they had at the time. My parents thought they were doing what was right, based on what they experienced growing up, and what they learned along the way. Today, there are more easily accessible resources on parenting.

Growing up was no walk in the park for me. I have already mentioned my father was a very angry individual. My mom did her best, but a lot of things were out of her control. My mom has been bipolar my entire life. She had a traumatic brain injury at the age of twenty-eight and was never the same. I remember being five years old and having to step in to help take care of my one-year-old brother while my dad tried to take care of my mom. The role of caregiver became more permanent as I reached my teenage years. There was a fine line between having a mom and mothering my mom. I digress and will save this story for Part III, Burnout.

For now, try to reflect on your inner critic and ask yourself, "When I hear this voice, who do I picture?" This may give you some insight to when you started to hear that voice. You may not picture a parent or caregiver from your childhood, but this question might open your mind to where these thoughts originally started. You likely didn't have a choice of how grown-ups in your life spoke to you as a kid, but as you begin to learn about your inner critic, you can change the words it uses.

SOCIAL CONDITIONING AND SOCIETAL EXPECTATIONS

You would think in 2022 that women wouldn't be facing the same issues as decades ago, but some issues still remain. Let's start with the beauty industry. A lot of pressure and stress are placed on young women to be, act, look, and think a certain way. Body image has been a point of contention for a long time. As a teen myself, teenage magazines portrayed anorexic women as the standard of beauty. I considered myself fat and overweight compared to the size 00s that swept magazine covers. Body positivity has changed immensely but it hasn't changed completely. Anti-aging cream,

Botox, and lip fillers are all promoted to enhance our beauty and keep our youth. When I was young, I just wanted to be older. Then when I got older, people around me said I needed to look younger.

Throughout my life I kept hearing conflicting views and didn't know who I should be listening to. "Be bold and assertive," they cheered, "but not too much because then people will think you're aggressive." "Be confident," they shouted, "but not too much because then men won't want to date you." "You should care what you look like," they announced, "but not too much because then you're vain and high maintenance." This was all so confusing.

Before we can even comprehend what is happening, girls and women are taught to be overly critical of themselves and to justify themselves when "no" is a sufficient answer. Women are taught to minimize their ambitions for fear someone will think they are bragging. Women are taught that we are each other's competition. Yet, I think society convinces us to fear each other because they know how powerful we can be when we are together and united.

For example, in 2018, the personal care products industry (which is heavily weighted with the beauty industry) accounted for $267.3 billion of the United States' gross domestic product.[4] That industry and the United States economy are held up by mascara, shampoo, and anti-aging creams. I know what you're thinking: "Well men have personal care products, too." You're not wrong; however, have you ever compared the prices? Products for women tend to be marked up substantially. But this is a different topic for a different day.

No wonder why I stumbled with my own inner voice as I was trying to navigate what society told me. I wanted to be beautiful, smart (not too smart), and liked because that's what society told me.

As a little girl, I was labeled a tomboy. I grew up with matching sweat pants and sweaters (before it became a thing during the

COVID-19 pandemic), and wore my sweats with my player number, depending on the sport of the season. I played field hockey, ice hockey, and rugby, attended a regional arts high school for piano, joined leadership conferences, and got high grades (except for English). I loved my black eyeliner and straight hair. I went to prom solo because no one asked, and I wasn't going to ask someone from a different school (I didn't want to entertain them the whole night because they wouldn't know anyone). On numerous occasions, even today, I have been told I'm intimidating and that's why men don't ask me out on dates. At seventeen, I didn't look like Britney Spears, or like Christina Aguilera from the "Dirrty" era. I didn't feel pretty or sexy. I was me, and I never felt enough.

Childhood, teenage, and young adult years are impressionable. We can't change what we went through, but we can change how we choose to move forward and how we alter that inner dialogue. When reflecting on your impostor beliefs and how they became deeply rooted in your subconscious, be kind to yourself. You may not know exactly how society's expectations affected your early formative years, ultimately affecting your adult years. Your younger self didn't know your subconscious was documenting and creating a narrative that would be used as ammunition later on. As you begin to pay attention to how you speak to yourself, be kind. You've been recording your voice this entire time.

CHAPTER 3

THE IMPOSTOR CYCLE

Let's recap: you are now aware of what impostor phenomenon (IP) is, how it came into existence, and why you continue to experience it. Now we will explore the *impostor cycle*. The impostor cycle is a series of steps that transpires after an initial thought that activates your stress response, awakening your inner critic, making you think everything has to be perfect (including you), causing you to either overwork or avoid and leads you to success each and every time. However, the cycle is repeated because your inner critic convinces you that you weren't good enough and dismisses your success.

The first time I read about the impostor cycle was in a book by Dr. Jessamy Hibberd.[5] Since then, I have thoroughly explored and adapted each step and checkpoint to help clients break free, because the impostor cycle resides in the depth of the subconscious and can be a trickster. It is sly, cunning, and crafty. It uses your inner voice and emotions against you. It makes you believe you aren't good enough and can never be good enough. The majority of the time, you don't even realize it's speaking because you've become accustomed to it.

I was sitting in a lecture hall of 300 students for a second-year physiology course during my undergraduate degree at age twenty. At this point in my career, I already knew I wanted to be a dentist so my only mission was to get the highest marks possible and get into dental school. I had horse blinders on, and it didn't matter what stood in my way. Within my horse blinders was my inner critic on full blast. It continued to motivate me the only way it knew how. *Those grades aren't good enough. What made you think you could get in to dental school? You're too much of a party girl. Go ahead, try studying, you're not going make it. You think you're smart? There are others who are better.* And it kept going on and on and on. I couldn't shut it off.

I snapped out of it when my professor shared a TED Talk. It was the first TED Talk I ever saw, called "Do schools kill creativity?" by Sir Ken Robinson, and let me tell you, I sat there with my jaw dropped the entire time. He spoke directly to me. I was constantly trying to suppress who I was, the creativity inside of me, in order to follow school rules, fit in, and get high grades because that is what North American society had deemed worthy. I struggled internally. In elementary school, there were times I was a distraction to the class, and the teacher would place my desk out in the hall so I wasn't disruptive. Instead of trying to figuring out why I was disruptive, it was easier to place me where no one else could see or hear me. Don't get me wrong, I understand trying to wrangle thirty students is challenging, but the twentieth century (and the twenty-first century) schooling system didn't account for the individual's learning style and interests. Leadership skills and creative thinking, which to me are important skills, become suppressed so students fall in line. Let me be very clear, do I think this is all teachers? Absolutely not. There are teachers I look back fondly on because they saw me for me and nurtured that.

In high school, I was more interested in committees and sports than I was in schooling. In university, it was the same. I found myself more intrigued with learning about leadership qualities than being in science classes. I should have stepped into those strengths, but I needed the science classes to become a dentist.

The decision to become a dentist was twofold. First, my aunt was a dentist, and I marvelled at her flexible schedule. In grade seven, when I had braces, she would take a day off work, take me to my appointment, and then we would come home and bake all day with her friends. I thought this was awesome. Second, society taught me that if you get a degree, then you'll be *successful.* I believed the propaganda, and at fourteen, the options available to me were: dentist, doctor, lawyer, accountant, and engineer. So, I made the decision early on and stuck to it. Looking at my parents and seeing how much they struggled, I saw dentistry as a way out of having any financial burden, but most of all, having safety—safety of a roof over my head, food on the table, the ability to travel, take care of the ones closest to me, to do the hobbies I want to do, buy what I want, and to be *happy*. This voice pushed me to strive for all of these things, but I lost my sense of who I was along the way.

Eleventh grade English class was an enormous struggle. I couldn't keep up with the readings. My test grades were low. I counted on group projects because I could use my creative thinking mind to craft without necessarily having to use the words and sentences part. That's where the help from my group members came in. Near the end of the semester our teachers would post our grades on the back of the classroom wall. A crowd of students would rush to the back and scramble around the sheet of paper, and even though the school tried, there was no anonymity. Everyone in the class knew what you got, and you really couldn't hide it. One day as we gathered around the back wall in English class, Brent, who stood next to me, saw my grade. I took a step back, not making eye contact. I saw his high-90s score sitting right next to my 65 and felt the shame seep through me.

The bell rang, and I ran out the door to advanced functions math class. Math felt safe for me even though Brent was in that class, too. It felt like I was having a déjà vu, because the teacher decided to post our grades as well. I skipped to the back of the classroom because I knew what these grades would be. High

90s; math was my forte. Numbers made sense to me. I could feel Brent's eyes on the back of my head as he approached from behind. He looked at his grade first and then scanned to mine and did a double take.

Brent turned rapidly toward me and said, "You're actually *smart?*"

My smile flattened. This was enough to feed my inner critic. *Actually . . . was I actually smart? Maybe I wasn't because I'm only good at math. Maybe that's not enough.* That should have been enough. I didn't know it at the time, and this is where the school system fails: not every class will be every student's strength, and unfortunately the system isn't set up to support students with their strengths so they can explore them further. Instead, students have to be good at all topics, otherwise there is a stain on their report card.

Fast forward to age twenty. I struggled not just in that physiology class but in all my second-year classes. It was one of the hardest years for me, not just because of the science courses but because I had an undiagnosed learning disability in reading comprehension that went unnoticed through high school. How did this happen? Because my high-90s grades in certain classes balanced out the mid-60s grades in classes with heavy reading, like English. But now that I was in university, everything had heavy reading.

That year I learned how to learn all over again. It was frustrating and infuriating. I felt ashamed and stupid. I wrote my exams in a separate room as I received extra time. This crippled my already dwindling confidence because I was different from everybody else. Yes, it answered why I struggled in school, but it didn't negate the fact that I officially didn't fit in. I knew higher academia didn't look fondly on learning disabilities, so how was I going to get into dental school? A low second-year grade point average and my new diagnosis would be stains on my application to dental school and on me as a human being. My inner critic started to become louder and louder. *This doesn't excuse why you had low grades. You're still stupid.*

That inner critic would take anything given to it and use it against me. It would twist and turn experiences to prove that no matter how hard I worked or how well I did, I was never going to be enough.

I continued to work hard no matter what was thrown my way. But I didn't just work hard. I pushed myself too far by signing up for multiple committees, pulling all-night study sessions, drinking the pain away (which I didn't know I was doing at the time), and overextending myself to prove my worth. Whether it was getting a good grade or being praised for a committee event, everything had to be perfect. If it wasn't perfect, then it was never good enough. I got decent grades, started a biomechanics master's program, managed my family dynamics, had good friends, and was in a relationship. That should have been success. But because my voice had cut me so many times, I couldn't see success anymore. I was going through the motions. I was stuck in the impostor cycle.

For the cycle to start, you are first pushed outside your comfort zone into a challenge, something new, or a life transition. This creates that uncomfortable feeling inside you: butterflies in your stomach, a lump in your throat, or what one of my clients has described as having ants in their pants. That feeling makes you question your capabilities and activate your inner critic, leading you to experience doubt and fear of failure. Your inner critic forces you to set extremely high standards and expectations, pushing you to strive for perfection. That drive demands the majority of your time and energy, causing you to overwork or avoid (a form of procrastination). Yes, procrastination takes up more time and energy than you can imagine (I'll explain why a little bit later).

In the end, whether you overworked or avoided, your achievement gets completed because you are a high achiever. Yes, even when you avoid or procrastinate, being that high achiever means you will reach your desired outcome . . . eventually. However, that success comes at a cost. The entire process was strenuous, and the cycle doesn't stop there. The final step is that the trickster makes you discount your success, eliminating any chance you may have to build and shape your confidence.

Below you will find a diagram of the impostor cycle. Together, we will break down each element. Along the way, I will teach you how to create checkpoints to stop you from repeating the same patterns, all while honing your confidence. In Part II and Part III, I'll build on the impostor cycle and give you more clarity about additional patterns including perfectionism and burnout.

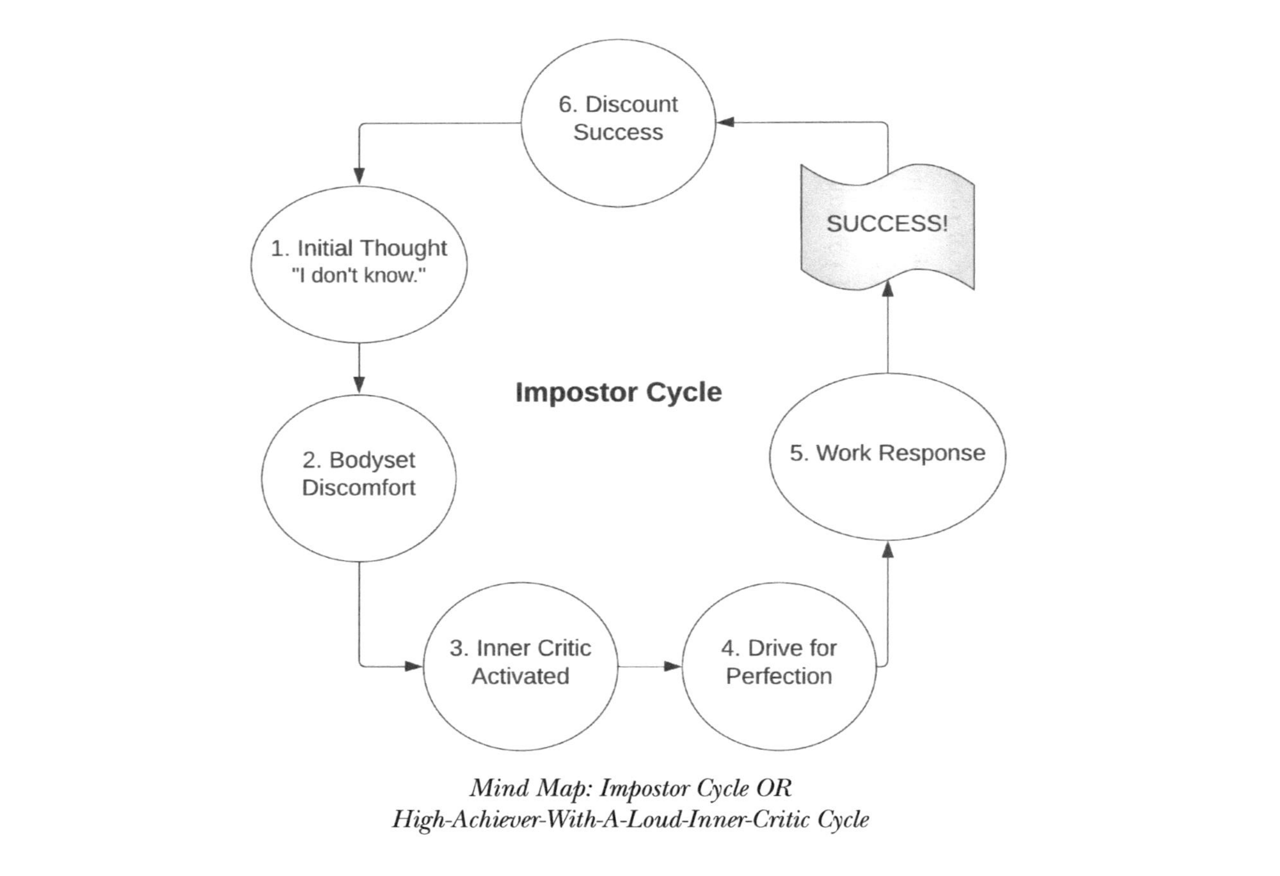

Mind Map: Impostor Cycle OR
High-Achiever-With-A-Loud-Inner-Critic Cycle

3.1 INITIAL THOUGHT

The first step in understanding how impostor phenomenon may be showing up for you is to pay attention to the initial thought that activates the cycle. It may be, "I don't know," or "I can't," or "I shouldn't," or "There is someone else who is better than me." That initial thought comes up when you are pushed outside your comfort zone, presented with a challenge or obstacle, or are starting something new, like a promotion or job. Paying attention to the initial thought allows you to develop self-awareness. **You can only change how you speak to yourself if you know what you are saying.** This is the first step in building a framework for your confidence to take shape.

When you drive to work with no music on, what are you saying? When getting ready for bed and taking your makeup off, what are you saying? When sitting at your computer writing an email, what are you saying?

Creating self-awareness is one of the hardest parts to making changes. When you start to listen to yourself you may not like what you hear and that's why you haven't paid attention. It's okay if you didn't realize what you were doing. I didn't either! We aren't taught to listen to our thoughts or understand our feelings. My early years taught me to suppress them, to hide them, and to not share. Being alone with my thoughts meant I would head down into darkness, which is not where I wanted to be.

I must have been around six years old. My parents had finished arguing, again. They usually argued behind closed doors, but it didn't matter. Door open or closed, the argument was always a screaming match that included some form of name-calling or an object being broken or even a fist through the wall. My brother and I would sit together or in our separate rooms, and I would sit and listen intently so I could try to fix things later.

On this specific day, my grandmother happened to call soon after the argument had ensued. I must have told her what was going on, which was then relayed to my father, because not long afterwards I was berated by him for sharing my feelings. The idea that sharing feelings is bad is an antiquated way of thinking. However, for six-year-old Jessica, that conversation with my grandmother about my feelings was the last time I ever shared my emotions until my cousin's death, fourteen years later (more on this in Part IV, Darkness).

It's important to listen to your voice and how you choose to speak to yourself because you hear your inner voice all the time. You may be someone who hears it as an inner monologue; or perhaps your thoughts are more visual. Not everyone speaks to themselves in first person. Some people speak to themselves in second or third person. You can hear your inner voice just as loud as though you were having a conversation with a friend because the same area of the brain gets activated.[6] Your brain can't tell the difference between a real conversation and an inner dialogue. Whether you say "I want a piece of toast" in your head or out loud, your brain hears it the same way. But it's not always that benign. If you say "I will never be good enough," it is just as real as though someone you trust is saying it to your face. Your brain believes your thoughts.

You may hear that same voice when you are reading in your head, rehearsing before a presentation, weighing different options, or playing out a future argument. We have all taken part in speaking to ourselves and activating that part of our brain. That voice is always having a conversation with you.[7]

Depending on who you speak to, you may use a different style of voice. Tone, pitch, pace, and volume may change based on the emotional connection and the point being discussed. If you speak to your pet, your voice may be high-pitched and, faster in speed, with a friendly or loving tone. If you speak to your partner in the bedroom, your tone may be gentle, slow, low, and sultry.

The same holds true with how you choose to speak to yourself. What tone, pitch, pace, and volume do you use to speak to yourself? What are the words you choose to use? Do you cheer yourself up to make yourself feel better or do you reprimand yourself, implying you're a constant failure? Your voice can boost your confidence, and it can cut your confidence down.

Your inner critic can be mean and full of believable lies. Your inner critic can judge you harshly. The words you use can be self-critical, demeaning, and hurtful. This is the opposite of your inner cheerleader. Your inner cheerleader is someone who brings you up, cheers you on, and inspires you. You likely know your inner cheerleader because you use it with your friends when they have a bad day. But when it comes to speaking to yourself, your inner cheerleader may be nowhere in sight. Without your inner cheerleader, it's difficult to find confidence.

Your inner voice has a massive effect on you as a human being, and as a high-achieving, high-performing, exceptional, powerful woman, the words you choose to use matter. "I'm not good enough," "I'm not worth it," I'm not perfect," "I can't," "I shouldn't," can have a profound impact on your emotional and mental well-being. This affects your actions, behaviours, and overall resiliency. It affects your ability to bounce back from challenges, to put yourself out there, and to not sit at home combing through every last detail of a past conversation. If you keep yourself stuck, then there isn't room to grow into your potential.

On an early Tuesday morning, in the dead of winter, I was curled into a fetal position in bed. The garbage can was next to me and the sheets thrown off. I lay sweating, profusely. I had food poisoning. I reached for the phone to call in sick. *They are going to think you're lying and being lazy.* Immediately, I sat up so fast the room started spinning. I dropped my phone and instead reached for the blue Gatorade, my eyes trying to find a spot in the room to focus on as my feet tried to find the ground. I took a sip. *This. Is. Ridiculous. You're being ridiculous. No one is going to think you're being lazy or lying. Enough.* There were brief moments, like having food poisoning, where my inner cheerleader spoke up against my inner critic. In this situation, I had to be extremely physically ill for my inner cheerleader to make herself known.

This became the turning point of when I started listening to how I spoke to myself. At the age of twenty-nine, it was as if I turned on a radio station to a horror story. How did I let my voice become so dark? How did I allow this to go on for so long? Why was the volume on so loud? And why couldn't I change the channel? I sat frozen in this awareness for months. I listened to this voice say destructive and hurtful things over and over again. I even listened as I justified why I said those things.

As time passed, I was angry with myself because it kept happening while all I did was sit on the sidelines, watching as this bully chewed me up and spit me out. I created a self-awareness but sat idly by. I became angry at myself that I couldn't catch myself fast enough from saying those hurtful words. **That's when I realized creating awareness was only the first step.** I decided it was time—time to make changes to that voice who haunted me for so many years. I knew this was going to be a challenge. I knew it was going to take time. I didn't know changing my inner narrative was going to take years because the pieces of my confidence were dispersed wide and far, deep in my subconscious.

As you start your self-awareness journey of listening for that initial thought, I suggest answering the questions below. Be as specific as possible. Allow yourself to pay attention to the voice. Notice when the voice is the strongest and loudest. **By documenting the voice, you will start to learn what the voice is saying, why it**

is saying such hurtful things, and when it occurs. Congratulations, you've begun the first step!

BRAIN TRAINING EXERCISE: SELF-AWARENESS QUESTIONS

1. When do you hear the negative voice? (Think time of day, day of week, time of month)
    - What do you say to yourself first thing in the morning?
    - What is the last thing you say to yourself before you go to bed?
    - When do you use words like "I can't" or "I shouldn't"?
2. How long does the voice last? (Seconds, minutes, hours)
    - Does the voice last longer when you are tired? Frustrated? Angry?
3. Who are you around? (Does someone or something activate the voice?)
    - Does an email, call, or text from someone in particular activate the voice?
4. What are you doing? (New project? Challenge? Working in a space that isn't a strength?)
    - What words do you use when stuck in a challenge?
5. Where are you? (Are you alone? At home watching TV? At work? Are you in bed getting ready to fall asleep?)

This is meant to be challenging. If you can't answer all the questions at once, start to move through your day, keeping these questions in mind. The more information you have, the better.

3.2 BODYSET/DISCOMFORT

Now that you're starting to get an idea of where these voices originated, it's time to figure out how they became trapped in your subconscious to be heard on repeat in the first place. This occurs through our mind-body connection known as the nervous system feedback loops.

For simplicity, a part of our nervous system can be separated into "flight-or-fight" (FF), "freeze" (FZ), and "rest-and-digest" (RD) responses. Your "fight-or-flight" and "freeze" response are a part of your stress response. Your "rest-and-digest" is a calming and more relaxed state of being. (A full explanation and a more science-y breakdown exists in Part III, Burnout). For right now, all I want you to understand is how the feedback loop works in regards to self-doubt and IP.

The moment you experience a challenge such as a new job and have that initial thought of "I can't" or "I don't know," you activate your FF response. When that happens, you begin to feel uncomfortable in your body: your heart beats faster, you sweat, you get a knot in your stomach and a lump in your throat. This is your body's way of responding to what you are currently thinking about. A chain reaction ensues. Your body's response wakes your inner critic, who shouts profound things and sets off IP, self-doubt, and fear of failure. In that exact moment, your mind and body connect IP with the body's discomfort. Your inner critic continues to convince you that you don't actually know what you're doing, and that pit in your stomach feels like it is telling the truth. There is no way to shut off this feedback loop if you always link that feeling of discomfort with your feeling of doubt. This means anytime you try something new and your body reacts through FF, you give your inner critic a full-on license to ground your plane and keep you stuck by repeating, "Yup, you're right, you're not good at all."

I know what you are thinking. How do I break the feedback loop? Even if it isn't easy, I promise you it's possible. **In order to break the feedback loop, you have to sit in the discomfort.** You have to analyze the discomfort, then tell your FF response you are safe to fly this plane, that you are qualified and capable. This creates a safe space for you to feel the discomfort and keep going. And just like with the initial thought, the first step is to pay attention. Each time you pay attention to your body's reaction, you will gather more information on how to navigate the discomfort, preparing you better for next time.

Unsure how to start? Don't worry, I got you! Here are some steps I've created to building this awareness:

Steps to understanding your bodyset and FF response:

1. Notice the discomfort. When you feel it, take a moment to reflect and recognize you feel uncomfortable.
2. What does it feel like? Be specific. Is it butterflies in your stomach? Is it an ache in your big toe? Do you feel like vomiting? When you are able to be specific, you begin to notice when your body has been activated by your inner critic, and you can determine whether or not your FF is absolutely necessary.
3. De-escalate your FF. To do this, remind yourself that you are, in fact, safe, that you aren't running for your life. Repeat the words, "I am safe." You can even try the 333 rule to bring you back to the present. Ask yourself, "What are three things I can see, three things I can smell, and three things I can feel?" (The "feel" is not emotions, but physical sensations). For example, you notice the sensation of the socks on your feet or hair on your shoulders. This brings you back to the present moment and reminds you that you are, in fact, safe and your FF response does not need to be switched on.

3.3 INNER CRITIC ACTIVATED

After the bodyset FF response is activated, your inner critic rears its head. I mentioned earlier that self-doubt is different from impostor phenomenon. However, your inner critic can use self-doubt against you. I'm not going to go into too much detail about your inner critic just yet because I have dedicated Part IV, Darkness, to speaking all about the narrative of the inner critic.

Here are a couple of details I think are important to know right now. A part of why your inner voice reminds you that you're not good enough is because it wants to protect you from feeling shitty. If that inner voice can keep you down and in the same place, then it has done its job of never letting you fail, but also never letting you feel successful or accomplished. It keeps the uncomfortable feelings away. **It thinks it is protecting you when, in fact, it is keeping you stuck.** If you were to try a new hobby and it didn't go as planned, then your inner critic can convince you to never try something new again. For now, as I take you through the impostor cycle, I want you to know that you can take the mic away from your inner critic. It doesn't have to be the only voice you hear, and this book will guide you through making those changes. Let's do this!

3.4 DRIVE FOR PERFECTION

When you start to hear your inner critic's voice, your drive for perfection gets activated. This is where your inner critic convinces you that perfection is the only thing that matters—not the desire to grow, the interest to learn something, or getting outside your comfort zone. The drive for perfection is about having a desire to control outcomes. If you can control the outcome, then you give yourself permission to feel successful, happy, or proud. Wanting perfection comes with struggles, as you will see in this section. In the next example, I'm going to show you how one of my client's worked through the initial thought, bodyset, inner critic, and drive for perfection.

Francesca, a client of mine, is a company executive who manages a small team and calls herself a perfectionist. She has years of work experience, a young family, and a three-year-old child. The first time I hopped on a call with Francesca, her voice was sweet and delicate, yet mighty.

I could hear her internal struggle: "I've tried everything and I just can't seem to get anything right. Why can't I do it perfect?"

One thing she had no doubt about in her mind was that she was a good mom—a tired mom, but a good mom. "I never have enough energy at the end of the day. When I get home, the little energy I do have, I spend complaining to my husband about work and how nothing went according to my plan. I see the frustration in his face because he keeps hearing the same story over and over." Francesca took a deep, exhausted breath. "I feel like I'm going in circles. I know I need to make a change but I don't know what it is, and that makes me feel overwhelmed. So then nothing changes."

This was becoming all too familiar. Client after client shared the same thoughts. They felt stuck, overwhelmed, and kept going in circles, expecting a change. The people they would confide in would tell them, "Keep going, it gets better." But all my clients questioned, "It gets better? How is it going to get better?"

With disappointment in their voices, my clients have said, "I can't keep living like this." What they didn't realize was they could control how they choose to speak to themselves.

Francesca's inner critic intensified how she was feeling. That voice had convinced her she should stay unhappy, stressed, and stuck because that's what she deserved because she couldn't reach perfection.

Together, Francesca and I started right at the beginning of the impostor cycle and began with creating self-awareness around how she chose to speak to herself. She was shocked with the number of times she heard herself say, "You're not good enough," in a day.

When she woke up, she would sit with her coffee, imagining how the day would unfold: *You know you're going to be too slow or make a mistake.*

When she got to work: *You're such a burden to the team.*

On the drive home: *You didn't do enough today.*

Francesca wanted perfection in everything she did, and when she felt like it wasn't enough, or it wasn't perfect, her inner critic reminded her that *she* wasn't enough.

After creating self-awareness, Francesca started to untangle her FF response. She found understanding her bodyset the easy part. She told me, "It makes me feel like shit. I feel like an elephant is crushing me and I'm only just trying to breathe. When the elephant sits on my chest, my inner critic pops up and solidifies my initial thought."

She was now aware of what she said to herself but it was her inner critic that made her feel like a constant, imperfect burden. It didn't matter if the people around her complimented her, because the thought was fleeting. It was easier to consider, *I'm not good enough, not perfect enough, for this job.*

When I asked Francesca why she thought she wasn't good enough for the job, she responded, "I just feel it. I know it."

I reminded Francesca that this was the feedback loop confirming suspicions about herself. The next step to breaking down the impostor cycle was to ask her inner critic specific and reasonable questions related to the challenge or project. Asking questions redirects your inner voice from shouting generalized statements like *I suck, I'll never be good enough, I shouldn't be the one to do this,* or *I'm a fake.*

Specific questions are critical to allow your mind to find fundamental answers, and the initial questions usually generate a set of sequential questions allowing you to explore further. Below is a list of sequential questions that can pop up if you are getting ready for that presentation, pitch, writing a book, job interview, difficult conversation, or any other situation that comes to mind. Instead of declaring the words *I'm going to suck,* substitute it for a relevant question and then answer it.

The Question	The Answer
"What if I'm not prepared?"	I have spent X days preparing. This is an adequate amount of time.
"What if I don't have the answer?"	I can find the answer. I can say in the meeting, "I don't know, let me get back to you."
"What if I fumble over my words?"	I am capable of picking up where I left off. I can keep going.

Reframing the generalized statement to a question allows your mind to settle because you gave it the opportunity to find an answer. Your mind is always searching for answers to the questions you give it, and the number of questions you ask yourself on any given day is plentiful. Whether it is asking what you are going to eat next or what investment you should make, your mind constantly ponders. It is when you find an answer that you give your mind permission to calm itself.[8] In general, your mind can think clearer when in a state of calm or neutral.

Now let's take this one step further and ask yourself, why do you really think you are not good enough? A part of you, your subconscious and your inner voice, knows what it really wants to ask but is too afraid to bring it forward. What you really want to ask yourself is, "How do I not suck, so I don't feel embarrassed or look stupid?" Am I right?

That inner voice is trying to convince you that feeling shame or embarrassment is bad and that you should avoid it at all costs. It tries to protect you but in a very convoluted way. So, you keep yourself stuck and avoid taking risks, avoid the possibility of stepping into what you are truly capable of, which is extraordinary awesomeness . . . if only you believed it.

Francesca started to reframe from generalized statements to specific questions. She noticed a change when her inner critic greeted her in the morning. Instead of immediately waking up and condemning herself before the day started, she was able to analyze what she was questioning and remind herself of her capabilities. This allowed her brain to calm down and start the day on a better note. This was a crucial step to harnessing her drive for perfection.

The drive for perfection becomes reinforced by setting unrealistic expectations. If it's not perfect, then it's a failure. It turns into a habit when you set unrealistic expectations and always assume you will never live up to them. Before you start anything, you convince yourself you won't be good enough. For high achievers, answering your thoughtful questions allows you to set realistic expectations.

You would think that if you set unrealistic expectations and meet them, then you would feel successful. However, when you are stuck in the impostor cycle, it isn't enough to reach those perfect unrealistic expectations. It is easier to condemn yourself for not raising the bar high enough. No matter the expectation, subconsciously you have already failed before even starting.

To set realistic expectations, Francesca and I looked at short- and long-term goals she wanted to achieve: stepping into a board room with confidence and getting promoted. We were then able to break down each goal to set realistic expectations. We designed a plan that looked at how to deal with setbacks, how to step into small successes, how to embrace discomfort, and when to reevaluate the expectations. It was no longer sufficient to rely on a feeling, because that feeling was being confused by her FF response and inner critic. The drive for perfection and setting unrealistic expectations can be broken down into five different impostor types: 1. The Perfectionist, 2. The Natural Genius, 3. The Expert, 4. The Lone Wolf, and 5. The Superwoman. Dr. Valerie Young[9] was the first person to describe each impostor type. Here, I share my interpretation of the impostor types, what I've seen with my coaching clients, and the helpful tips I have created to go with each.

1. THE PERFECTIONIST

The perfectionist looks at how something gets done. She aims to always reach perfection, striving for a hundred out of a hundred. No, this isn't a test, this is the goal she sets unrealistic expectations for. The perfectionist doesn't believe in celebrating her successes because her capabilities are never good enough. If the entire circumstance renders a 99 percent, the perfectionist only sees the 1 percent that was out of reach. She deems the circumstance a failure. The perfectionist is blinded by that one mistake, that one hang-up, that one thing that contributed toward the goal not being a hundred percent successful. The drive for perfection is not for the hope of success but for fear of failure.

Alex, another one of my clients, couldn't see anything she did right. She kept setting goals and achieving them but nothing was ever good enough, and she felt like it could have always been better. I asked her to describe in phases the last goal she set, the implementation phase, and the outcome. Alex recounted a project she pitched to her bosses month ago. The project was to change internal systems, which would help with efficiency and flow of the day, giving employees more time to spend on tasks with higher priority.

The implementation phase came with challenges. People resorted back to old ways, the flow became disjunct, and colleagues complained constantly. Eight months later, the new system was in place and not only was Alex complimented, but they held a celebratory gathering to congratulate her. Alex didn't see her accomplishment or her success. At the celebration, she kept talking about all the problems that transpired and disqualified the resulting success.

She discounted her hard work, critical thinking, and problem-solving abilities because of the obstacles along the way. It was easier to focus on the unforeseen complications than it was to see the progress or opportunities to adjust and allow for improvements. It can be difficult to remind yourself of the long-term vision when you get bogged down in day-to-day shitstorms.

Alex and I unpacked the eight months: the ups and downs, the lefts and rights, and everything in between. For every adversity she shared, I offered an alternative outlook without dismissing how she felt about the situation. By changing Alex's perspective, it gave the perfectionist in her the permission to change her narrative to recognize her current and acquired skills. She began to witness her strengths and abilities, and this changed how she saw her role in the project and how she felt about herself. I am still shouting from the rooftops, "You go, Alex!"

HELPFUL TIPS FOR THE PERFECTIONIST IMPOSTOR TYPE

1. Be specific with your goal setting. Get simple, tangible, and practical. This allows for you to accurately measure what you achieved. Focus on the process and your progress instead of only getting through to the end result. When you're setting a long-term or a big, uncomfortable goal that makes you stretch, you still have to go back to the smaller goals that help you work towards that bigger goal.
2. Be realistic about unforeseen obstacles. There is no way any one person can think of all the possible negative outcomes that can happen. You can, however, prep yourself for how you choose to respond when obstacles and challenges appear. Go into your next goal knowing something will go wrong but you will be able to figure it out when it happens. You have the knowledge to be able to problem solve.

2. THE NATURAL GENIUS

The natural genius looks at how and when something gets done. She measures her success by ease and speed. If she can't grasp a talent, skill, or project on the first try, she considers it a failure, drops it like a hot potato, and criticizes herself. This woman may or may not notice she gives up too soon and avoids taking risks. Setbacks can throw her off her game entirely, thinking she isn't smart enough.

Alex, the same client as above, took me through each phase of her project. "Wait," you may be wondering, "can you be more than one impostor type?" The answer: yes, yes you can. I'll explain this a little bit later. Alex connected with being a perfectionist and a natural genius. From the idea, to implementation, to outcome, she would become easily distraught if she or someone on her team didn't learn something fast enough. She would get frustrated and say, "I'll just do it," and then she would blame herself for a task not getting done or not being perfect.

Throughout the project, I had Alex explore the setbacks she described to determine whether they were true setbacks due to unforeseen circumstances and out of her control, or if they were setbacks defined by the natural genius's unrealistic expectations. I helped Alex shift her perspective once again instead of only seeing the negative or thinking the worst-case scenario. Alex began to see the opportunities even when it wasn't going exactly as planned. This included finding a new pace at work during the growth phase.

I commended Alex for not giving up, because it is easy to either do it yourself or walk away altogether. As you become proficient in set skills, you forget how long it can take to learn something new, and that is what happened here for Alex. She forgot about her already existing skills, how they could be applied, what it takes to learn something new, and that sometimes unexpected challenges arise. Alex and I spoke about future ideas so the most recent project wouldn't be the reason she chose not to keep doing new things. She documented, yes, documented, because I told her to write them all down, all the skills she learned so she remembers them for the next project.

HELPFUL TIPS FOR THE NATURAL GENIUS IMPOSTOR TYPE

1. Don't give up after the first try . . . or second, or third. Keep trying. Keep at it. Find your strength within this challenge.

Acknowledge the skill it takes to learn something different or new altogether. Commend yourself on the progress, looking at how far you have come instead of only focusing on how far you have to go.

2. Start small, and do one thing at a time. The brain underestimates and devalues daily consistent practice. If you're learning something new or are stuck in an obstacle, a little bit each day goes a long way.

3. THE EXPERT

The expert looks at what and how much she knows or can do. It is the knowledge version of the perfectionist, which means the perfectionist thinks she must do everything perfectly while the expert thinks they must know everything before starting or putting herself out there. She condemns herself if she doesn't have the answers. She speaks down to herself, *If you were really smart, you would have already known this.* When she doesn't know something, she considers it a failure. This woman can get stuck in the information stage, also known as analysis paralysis. She is always writing to-do lists, always doing more research or taking another course before thinking she is capable and skilled.

"But what if someone asks me a question and I don't know the answer?" Lucy asked in one of our sessions.

I answered the question with a question. "What if you don't know the answer?"

Lucy sighed. "They'll think I'm stupid and don't know anything."

I paused while I heard the crack in Lucy's voice. It always came back to this statement of stupidity and the feeling of inadequacy and risk of humiliation. She felt like she needed to know everything because someone would question if she was smart enough or if she belonged in her role. Lucy and I spent time working through this one specific thought and how to change not only how she viewed herself, but how she thought others viewed her. It always came back to whether or not she felt intelligent. Lucy would put off applying for new jobs and implementing new strategies because she felt she was never going to have enough information to adequately deliver.

HELPFUL TIPS FOR THE EXPERT IMPOSTOR TYPE

1. Start small and get going. You do not need to know everything. You aren't expected to know everything. You are expected to know what you know right now and to continue to grow. When you know different, you do different. But until then, you may have to start and figure some things out along the way.
2. Connect with information you already have and know. Lean into your existing knowledge. Every bit of information and skill you have is completely transferable. You just have to figure out how. You are never starting from scratch again; even if you are learning something brand new, you likely have a skill that can be implemented with it.

4. THE LONE WOLF

The lone wolf looks at who completes the task. She thinks she must do everything, from sending out reminder emails to calling clients to say thank you to running a board meeting. She considers asking for help as weakness. She struggles with setting boundaries and is always overworking. She chooses to do everything on her own because she is the only one who can do it perfectly, and if she gives it to someone else, she knows it won't be perfect. She thinks it's a waste to tell someone else what to do because she'll eventually have to do it herself, again.

Malia felt like everything had to be perfect at work. Her emails, perfect. Her conversations, perfect. Her schedule, perfect. Her referrals, perfect. Her procedures, perfect. There was no room for error. On one of our coaching calls, she was interrupted twice in the matter of thirty minutes by her office, because she had primed her office to ask her about every detail. She removed their ability to problem solve, have autonomy, and trust their own judgement.

Her employees weren't given the opportunity to grow from mistakes or find solutions to even minor problems. She had stunted her staff by doing everything and thinking she had to do everything by herself.

Malia and I spent months learning how to delegate tasks and teach her employees, so she could build their self-confidence and trust in their abilities. We started small, like not reviewing every referral that went out. If it had a spelling mistake or was sent back with questions, they were then able to improve for the next time. Malia had to figure out what was small enough to start with and grow into delegation.

HELPFUL TIPS FOR THE LONE WOLF IMPOSTOR TYPE

1. Ask for help. Don't wait until you have no energy or are completely burnt out to ask for help. If you are at your wit's end, you are past the point of when you should have initially asked for help.

2. ASK FOR HELP. Yes, this one I have to repeat, and I'm also repeating for my own benefit. Start small in an area that can be communicated easily, and delegate that task. You should be putting your time and energy into things that really only you can do and are strong at. Lean on team members and others to use their strengths as well.

5. THE SUPERWOMAN

The superwoman looks at how many roles they can be perfect at. This is the perfectionist on overdrive. Being perfect has overflowed into her personal life. She is constantly "on" and may even feel chronically tired. This woman feels like she doesn't just have to be the best boss or employee, but she also needs to be the best mom, daughter, partner, athlete, mentor, volunteer, and baker. Being a perfectionist no longer suffices just at work. The superwoman needs to be outstanding in all aspects of her life. This woman feels like rest is for the weak. If she tries to take a break, she feels guilty she isn't achieving something on her to-do list. There is always something on the to-do list.

Kiara was extremely high energy. She had everything organized immaculately because she believed it was the only way she was able to do everything. However, at times, she felt like she wasn't good at anything. She put so much pressure on all aspects of her life that she didn't give herself the flexibility for life to evolve right in front of her eyes. She knew her perfectionism wasn't sustainable long-term.

Kiara sighed and described a day when she had run out of her daughter's favourite bread. "I left work at eight o'clock and immediately drove to the grocery store. But when I got there, they were closed. I drove to the next grocery store, and they were closed, too. I started to get nervous thinking I'm a crappy mom because I can't even get my daughter's favourite breakfast right."

I asked, "Do you have other breakfast items in the house?"

"Of course," she scoffed.

"Will she eat the other breakfast items?"

"Yes, but, I couldn't get her *favourite* breakfast." Kiara took a deep breath. "What kind of mom can't get her daughter bread?"

I knew there was more going on. It wasn't about the bread. Kiara was overextended. Her capacity to be perfect at everything was creating tension for herself, her husband, her little girl, and her office. Kiara and I leaned into setting realistic expectations that allowed for down time as well. She worked on feeling less guilty around imperfections and things that were out of her control. Along the way, she built self-compassion around the challenges that presented. This was no easy feat and would be an ongoing process throughout her life. However, Kiara knew stepping into being the best mom she could be, instead of the perfect superwoman, was worth it.

HELPFUL TIPS FOR THE SUPERWOMAN IMPOSTOR TYPE

1. Switch off for five minutes. Start there. I'm not saying you need to put everything on hold and take a vacation. I'm only saying to take five minutes to sit still, drop your shoulders, and take a breath.
2. Create a scheduled break. Block off time in your calendar just as if you were booking yourself an appointment to see the dentist or doctor. Create time in your schedule for yourself and make it a priority. When you can block off that time, not only is it something to look forward to, but it takes

pressure off of trying to find random times throughout a week to "fit" in time for you or self-care.

Now let me ask you this: which impostor type did you resonate with? Did you notice you have overlapping characteristics? I can reassure you it's okay to resonate with more than one impostor type, just like Alex. For myself, I related immensely to the superwoman and the expert. I can catch myself getting stuck in analysis paralysis and noticing my perfectionist tendencies seep into other aspects of my life, including playing sports and hosting a dinner party. The importance in knowing your impostor type is so you can create self-awareness and start applying the helpful tips. It's all about recognizing what isn't working for you, then slowly starting to implement modifications to get unstuck from the impostor cycle. We will fully dive into perfectionism and how it all connects as a branch to the impostor cycle in Part II.

3.5 WORK RESPONSE (OVERWORKING AND AVOIDANCE)

For those who experience impostor cycle, there are two types of responses to how they choose to use their time and energy: to overwork or avoid. *Overworking* is spending an enormous amount of time and energy on any and all tasks. It's fiddling over the size of a font in a presentation, redoing your own work because it wasn't exactly perfect, spending more hours at the office when you don't need to be there, taking work home, beating yourself up on the drive home, thinking about what you need to do before you go to bed, and waking up in the middle of the night anxious about what you have to do. All of these things are a form of overworking. A large reason for overworking is to help calm your FF response in the short term. You've convinced yourself that spending that extra hour nitpicking will be the only reason you are successful. **Overworking is the proof you use to define your success and worth.**

When you overwork, you don't give yourself the opportunity to explore what happens when you *don't* overwork. It also means you almost never have enough time for rest, relaxation, recovery, or fun. The way you feel is an afterthought, and your success is defined by how exhausted you are.

Overworking, by North American society, has been glamorized (moving forward, anytime I mention society or culture, because I live in Canada, I will be referring to North American society and culture). The propaganda of women "having it all" means you have to burn the candle at both ends in order to be successful. Work hard at work, then work hard at home, then work hard trying to be fit and healthy, and work hard to have it all. When I was stuck in the impostor cycle, I was stuck glamorizing overworking. In fact, I wore it as a badge of honor.

This way of working can lead to cyclical crashes. Work, work, work until the goal is met, and then crash for a few days (or months) until you have the next goal to work toward. How many times have you pushed yourself to the limit, only to get to a vacation and not really enjoy it because you are too tired or became sick? How long does it usually take for you to settle into your vacation? How many times have you returned from a vacation thinking it was a waste because you don't feel any better? If you answered yes to one or more of these questions, then you are likely overworking and self-sabotaging. And get this, it doesn't just apply to vacation; this includes weekends, evenings, and any down time you take for yourself.

The crash that happens after you have overworked is your body's response to the rapid decline of adrenaline you have been living on for too long.[10] I have experienced this on too many occasions, repeating the cycle over and over again. I could tell you exactly when I would get sick: after the end of a big project, at Christmas, and at the start of vacations. I accepted this for what it was and assumed I would always have to live like this, always planning around the first part of a vacation knowing I would be sick. How did I deem that acceptable? Planning around planned sickness because I made myself sick?

I lived like this for a very long time because my inner critic had me convinced I couldn't live up to those unrealistic expectations. I scolded my body for betraying me. *How could you get sick?* I belittled myself, and it didn't even occur to me that was something within my control—how I was choosing to speak to myself.

Another way to expend time and energy without even realizing you are doing it, is through *avoidance* or procrastination. For most high-achieving women, when we hear the word *procrastination,* we relate it to being lazy. I want to be very clear when I say this: you are NOT lazy. You do not procrastinate because you are lazy. You avoid or procrastinate because you are putting off the uncomfortable feeling that bubbles to the surface when your inner critic reminds you of your doubts and fears. **Avoidance is a temporary time and energy relief that allows you to avoid discomfort.**

Here's the problem: you will eventually have to give the presentation, have that conversation, or quit that job. The challenge will still be there lingering in the background. You may have put it off, but your subconscious doesn't put it off. Your subconscious goes through scenarios in the background while you're working on something else. At times you may feel a pit in your stomach, get woken up in the middle of the night, or feel like you can't relax. Even though you're not actively thinking about the challenge, your subconscious doesn't realize that, which means you never truly rest. This gives your inner critic the license and opportunity to sneer, "*Well, lazy pants, another thing you haven't done. No wonder why you're not going anywhere.*" This isn't conducive to building confidence. In fact, it's the complete opposite.

When you avoid challenges, you program yourself to think you can only get something done if you leave it until the last minute. Your FF gets activated and you power through, maybe even pulling an all-nighter. Remember, success follows. You label yourself a procrastinator and accept that's who you are. Imagine how drained your subconscious mind is always thinking about the to-do's, always on the alert but never stepping in. It's like a soccer player on the side of the field, ready on their toes, waiting for the signal from the referee, always waiting, and never knowing when.

Whether you find yourself overworking or avoiding, an important strategy to help make these changes is to implement time blocks for the work you would like to accomplish. If you overwork, set a realistic amount of time and step away when the time block is over. Give yourself permission to stop and move on to the next task, take a break, or go step out into the sun. You will become more efficient during the time blocks.

Michelle, one of my clients, owns her own business in project management. A part of her job as CEO is reviewing finances once a month with her accounting team. This was something she knew was important but absolutely despised. She would put it off or schedule a meeting last minute, affecting both her and everyone else's schedule. At times, it followed her home on weekends and evenings because she would put it off until the last possible minute. Michelle knew she was avoiding it because going over numbers made her feel uncomfortable.

As an aside, a lot of women have shared the same sentiment with me: not wanting to look at bank account statements or review personal or professional finances because it makes them nervous and agitated. I've given keynote speeches to women financial organizations, and they tell me they notice it among their clients, too. The same finance women also say that the financial industry is still male-dominated and there aren't many women in leadership roles. Sara Connell, author of *The Science of Getting Rich for Women,* wrote, "The pandemic has cost women $800 billion dollars in lost income globally," and that is a massive number.[11] So, my question is: what if women weren't afraid of money?

Well, for Michelle, we implemented two time blocks per month dedicated to reviewing finances on her own and with her team. I had Michelle do it for six months. That meant at the end of the six months she would have met with her team twelve times. I suggested two times per month with shorter time blocks rather than one larger time block, but you can figure out what works for you. Shorter time blocks help reduce the FF response around having to be uncomfortable for such a long period of time. Also, I wanted to expose Michelle to stepping into that discomfort more often so she'd know she could separate the mind-body connection and pay attention to her inner critic.

Carving out these time blocks in Michelle's schedule helped reduce the subconscious energy expended from overanalyzing or overthinking leading up to the reviews, and it structured her schedule so she wasn't taking work home or having it overflow into her weekends and beyond. Michelle still implements this strategy and has started to apply it with her personal finances as well!

One massive rule you must stick to is: avoid multitasking during the time blocks. If you dedicate a set of two hours to writing an article, then you must write the article. You can't check social media, your emails, and answer the phone at the same time. When you constantly switch back and forth, it can take, on average, approximately twenty-three minutes to get your focus back on the original task.[12] That means if you are always multitasking, you are never truly focused on what requires your attention. It's using up way more of your energy and time.

Time Block Example: Putting together a presentation, social media post, paper, or event:

Look back at the last presentation you gave. Let's say you spoke for twenty minutes but it took you seven hours to put it together; where did you spend your time? If you spent an hour picking out colours and design, two hours for the body of it, two hours editing fonts and images, and two hours rehearsing, look at where you can cut time.

You can cut time on picking out colours and editing. If you combined and cut colours, design, and editing into an hour, you get back two hours. That may not seem like a lot, but two hours adds up over time. That's two extra hours to rest, get a massage, play with your kids, watch your favourite show, or call your best friend. The high-achieving woman will easily find an activity to do with that time. And, that's the beauty of it— you get to decide where you really want to spend that time. I know that's unheard of. But really, you can.

To summarize, if you find yourself procrastinating, setting time blocks helps by reducing the amount of time and energy spent on a task. I'm not just talking about when you actively complete the task during the time block, but also the time and energy spent thinking about what you have to do. Time blocks give your subconscious mind time to rest. When I procrastinate, I picture my inner critic pulling up a comfy couch and tossing a piece of popcorn into its mouth, one at a time, as it sits there spewing dreadful words and watching me squirm. Add the time blocks, and the inner critic doesn't have anywhere to sit or anything to eat. It stays quiet and doesn't scold you.

3.6 DISCOUNTING SUCCESS

Let me remind you, you will always be successful as the high achiever who experiences impostor phenomenon (IP) and travels through the impostor cycle. You may overwork or avoid (or do both), but success is waiting for you and wondering when you will celebrate it. Success is a perspective. You choose how to view it, interpret it, and embrace it. Just as you decide to discount yourself, you have the power to own success and happiness, fully stepping into both. You know you have spent months and likely years working toward your goal, and yet you negate it in one fell swoop. Stepping into success for the woman who experiences the impostor cycle is difficult.

If you overworked, you will look back and think about the amount of time and energy you put in and that you will never be able to do it again. You think you won't be able to attain the same level of satisfaction because the levels of effort were unsustainable. Yet, when it comes time to entertain a new challenge, you slip back into old ways.

If you procrastinated, it becomes easy to explain why something didn't live up to your expectations. It gives you an excuse to say, "Well, I left it until the last minute; that's why it wasn't that good," explaining away your current success. Time and time again, whether you overworked or avoided, your inner critic is given the opportunity to run wild, grabbing at any new information to remind you that you are not good enough and will never be.

In May 2015, I walked into Metcalf Auditorium at Boston University with a selfie stick raised high, documenting it all. It was graduation day. No, the auditorium wasn't named after my family; it was a mere coincidence that definitely made me smile.

It was time to get called up on stage to accept my doctor of dental medicine degree. As I got closer to the stairs, I could feel the nerves rising up and my thoughts racing. *Will I grab the degree and shake the dean's hand in the right order? Did I wear the right shoes? Will I be the one who trips on stage?*

I actually don't remember walking across the stage. I do remember sitting in my chair, gripping my degree so tight I thought it would bend. *Now what?* I asked myself. I was already starting to worry about the next thing: *Will I be a good dentist? Did I choose the right residency program? How many years should I be an associate before I buy an office?* I didn't stop to savour my success. In seconds, I discounted a lifelong achievement of mine. In seconds, I discounted the last eleven years with two words: *Now what?*

It was so easy to discount my success and so hard to own it because I was stuck in the impostor cycle without even knowing. I hardwired my brain to accept successes as being trivial components in my life. These successes were just one more thing to get done because it would always be the next thing that would finally make me smart enough. But that next thing would never actually arrive. This is called moving your success over the cognitive horizon. In *The Happiness Advantage*, written by Shawn Achor, he describes this in detail.[13] I'll sum it up here: when we continue to move our success or happiness over the cognitive horizon, we never actually reach it. This is similar to moving your goal post without noticing how far you have come. If you don't give yourself the opportunity to embrace and acknowledge your achievements, successes, or happiness, then it doesn't matter what you are trying to accomplish. You will never feel enough, and that goal you were trying to achieve will always be just out of reach.

When you stay stuck in the impostor cycle, you hardwire your brain to believe success is unattainable and that you'll never be good enough. This path confirms that the impostor cycle is the only way to live. It becomes familiar, too familiar, and eventually it is the only accepted route. Each time reinforces the belief that your inner critic must motivate you, that you have to strive for perfection, that you need to either overwork or procrastinate. And in the end, you ultimately discount your success.

If you try to step outside the cycle, it can feel so uncomfortable that it becomes easier to slip back. But your mind is constantly learning and evolving, if you allow it. This is where you can rewire that hardwired circuit and step outside of the cycle. It takes time and practice but it is totally worth it. This is why it is important to savour your successes.

Women, in general, have a hard time sharing their successes for fear of what others might think or say about them. It's easier to justify success instead of embrace it. How many times have you explained yourself after receiving a compliment? "Oh, you know, I had Donna's help to actually make this happen," or "Well, I was just lucky because it all came together." No, woman! It was because of *you*! Take the compliment; say thank you. And if there's a silence after the thank you, then live in the discomfort of the silence. Resist the urge to fill the silence with a justification. It's time to own your successes. Believe in them. Share them with the world, and most of all, savour them.

If you feel like it's bragging, it's not—at least, not for the woman who experiences IP. You can share your successes in ways you feel comfortable. You don't need to post it on social media, you don't need to share it with just anyone, but you do need to savour it. Pick people you feel comfortable sharing with and who will be delighted for you. Print that testimonial and hang it on your wall. Jot it in your journal. Take a picture of yourself in the moment you witnessed your own success. Stand in front of the mirror and point at yourself and say, "Ya, you fucking did that." This is how you savour your successes, by relishing in the glow of what you've accomplished.

When you savour your success, two things happen. First, when you talk about it more, it becomes a stronger memory to pull on in the future. Second, when you notice your successes, you start to see them in other places. This is known as frequency illusion or the Baader–Meinhof phenomenon.[14] A common example of the phenomenon occurs with shopping. Let's say you decide to buy a new car, a blue Tesla to be specific. Because you have brought this forward to your attention, you'll notice that more people in your neighbourhood or out on the roads are driving a blue Tesla, the exact same car you now want.

Unfortunately, the same holds true for negative experiences or emotions. One of the reasons they are more prominent in our memory banks is because of the way the negative experiences make us feel. You can't tell me you don't have one of those memories every once in a while, where a thought comes forward and you are reminded of a past moment that makes you cringe. Our brain is hardwired to protect us physically, emotionally, and mentally from danger, shame, humiliation, and embarrassment. Cringeworthy moments are uncomfortable because the mind-body connection doesn't want you to live in your FF response; it wants to prevent it. Our mind collects these memories throughout our life to protect ourselves, to hopefully predict and prevent another cringeworthy moment.

Imagine the power we'd have if we applied this same principle to our successes! If you applied the same conditions to savouring your success, then you can replicate the confidence you had from past success. Whenever you encounter a new challenge, you can remind yourself of past successes and step into that confident feeling. It proves you are knowledgeable and have done it before. Thus, you can do it again!

It was a usual day in clinic for me. I had just given local anesthetic to one of my patients and headed back to my office to write chart notes. I usually put my phone on "do not disturb" because I hate when my smart watch goes off in the middle of procedures. Today, I forgot.

As I headed back to clinic, my wrist began buzzing. I looked down at my watch and it was Anika, a client of mine. Anika is a wealth financial advisor. She has been one for over a decade. It was odd, as my coaching clients know when I'm in clinic so they usually send texts or emails. I instantly knew something was wrong.

I picked up the phone, and, before Anika started speaking, I heard tears. "Jess, I can't do this. What if I don't live up to their expectations? What if I can't produce? What if I'm the wrong person for this job?"

Anika had shared on social media that she was promoted and that her new role specifically was to empower more women within the same male-dominated financial industry I mentioned previously.

Her post went viral. She couldn't keep up with how fast people commented. The responses were compliments and praise, yet Anika had this pit in her stomach.

"I'm such a fake. It's only a matter of time before they find out."

By now, I was sitting back at my desk. I responded gently. "Anika, tell me what people wrote on the post."

She proceeded to share the compliments and excitement from others.

"Anika, tell me why empowering women is important to you."

She told me about the women who were stuck in marriages and jobs they hate, that they felt stuck because they didn't know enough about money. Anika's mission is to help women become financially literate so they can ask for raises, learn how to invest, manage risk tolerance, and own their money.

"Anika, tell me why you are good for this job."

She described how passionate she felt about helping these women and making a difference in society.

"Anika, tell me why you believe you can do this."

After a short pause: "Because I have a voice. I know I can do this. I know my message and mission."

I could hear the power return to her voice. The tears stopped.

"I definitely can do this."

I beamed. "You most definitely can!"

This is an example of Socratic questioning used in the form of savouring and establishing someone's success. Socratic questioning is when a coach helps a client reflect on an experience by asking a series of focused, open-ended questions to create awareness through a different perspective. I could have hopped on this call with Anika and praised her and told her how amazing she was, but she likely wouldn't have believed it and would still have thought she couldn't do it. Instead, I guided Anika into finding past evidence so she could clearly visualize her capabilities and could believe in herself. Socratic questioning is something you can practice on your own as well. Ask yourself open-ended questions instead of allowing your inner critic to tell you that you can't do something. This, too, takes practice but is well worth it.

It's easy to underestimate yourself when you don't give yourself permission to savour your success. In that split second, Anika experienced IP to the fullest extent. Because she was stuck in speaking negatively about herself, she couldn't find the evidence, the words, and perspective to change her opinion about herself. Her initial thought of "I can't do this" activated her FF response so strongly she was ready to fight or fly. That adrenaline rush was such a profound feeling Anika couldn't summon her inner cheerleader.

Savouring success is an important part of reflection. Reflection is when you acknowledge and give yourself permission to own your success and establish how to use it for growth. It allows you to understand the areas requiring improvement without discounting your abilities. When your inner critic is shouting from a megaphone, it becomes challenging to manage that voice and slips you right into rumination. Rumination is different from reflection and is what happens when you only review what went wrong, keeping you stuck and reminding you of all the negatives. Rumination doesn't allow you to grasp present achievements, the progress you have made, or your fullest potential.

Well, we have made it one full turn around the impostor cycle, and I want to do a quick recap. Notice your initial thought and what your bodyset is doing during your FF response. Pay attention to how your inner critic speaks to you and what your inner critic is saying. When you step into demanding perfection, assess what impostor type may be holding you stuck and notice whether you step into overworking or avoidance. Then, notice what you tell yourself when you discount your success. Knowing what you do during all these steps is huge. When you create awareness at each step, it gives you the opportunity to try out some of the helpful tips I provided along the way.

Are you going to master all the changes on the first go? Likely not, but that's okay. It will take time. Along the way, you get to figure out what works best for you. As a reminder, if you get stuck in one of the steps and it takes a while to navigate through, don't slip back into beating yourself up, but sprinkle a little bit of self-compassion, because, damn it, you're evolving.

CHAPTER 4

THE IMPORTANCE OF INTERNAL VALIDATION

How you choose to speak to yourself impacts your mental, physical, and spiritual well-being. It can bring you up on days when you feel down, but it can also tear you down on days you feel good. It can even kick you when you are already down. Days when you feel more emotions or have had a sleepless night are opportunities for your inner critic to come barreling in, screaming profanities at you. Despite how you feel, you have the choice to nourish yourself by choosing kinder and nonjudgmental words, which is a form of internal validation.

In *Think Again* by Adam Grant, he discusses the silver lining behind experiencing IP: the motivation to work harder than anyone around you, the openness to new ways of doing things, and becoming a better learner. In a recent workplace study conducted by Basima Tewfik, she concluded that individuals who experience IP were able to perform the task at hand without work being negatively impacted.[15] In particular, these individuals became more others-focused, which means they had better interpersonal skills like being an active listener, showing empathy, and engaging in more inquisitive questions. However, Tewfik does share in an interview with Time.com that the research isn't exactly clear and straightforward, which means that just because results showed better interpersonal skills doesn't mean we should disregard when someone is being negatively impacted by impostor thoughts. Just as I described in the first part of the book, people who really sink into IP often get stuck in the impostor cycle and can't get out.

Okay, so there we have it. IP can be good and push you outside your comfort zone, but it can also be extremely detrimental and keep you stuck in your comfort zone. I think a significant component that determines if you stay trapped is how you choose to speak to yourself and build internal validation. If your own voice, your inner critic, credits your success to luck, reminds you of only your failures, tells you to overwork to prove your worth, downplays your achievements, and holds you back from thinking you can reach a desired goal, then it will forever keep you in a comfort zone making you feel not enough. But is that where you want to stay? In a place full of dislike toward yourself?

At times, it may seem inconsequential when you say things like, "Oh man, I suck," which I heard from one of my past colleagues on a phone call. Or when I even caught my own accountability partner hopping on our weekly video call saying, "I'm a loser; I didn't do my homework this week." Your subconscious doesn't realize you're saying it as a joke. Your subconscious thinks you're a loser.

When I heard my accountability partner say it, my eyebrow lifted, and she replied, "Fiiine. I know."

"You know what?" I asked.

"I'm not a loser. I'll reframe. I didn't have time and chose to prioritize other tasks. That's why I didn't complete my homework."

I grinned. "Much better."

It can honestly be that simple.

Just like with Anika, it would have been easy for me to tell her she wasn't a loser, but that doesn't help her build her own internal validation. She had to remind herself and do the reframing.

Throughout our lives, the inner critic has made its grand entrance, strutting its thing, being the loudest, and evoking intense, deep-rooted emotions. This voice has used words that sound familiar and natural but are harsh and demeaning.

I vividly remember looking out the front window of my family's house when I was about fourteen years old. I waited for my friends to come and pick me up and go to the movies. This was before the era of text messaging or cell phones, so I waited there and wondered: *They probably forgot about me because they don't like me. I'm not that pretty anyhow. Argh, I'm so stupid. How could they want to be my friends?*

Throughout my life, there were days I looked at my reflection in the mirror and picked apart every single flaw, not just physical, but mental and emotional as well. I would have settled for a voice that said, "Daaaamn, you're pretty awesome! How did you get to this stage in your life?" or "I'm not 100 percent sure you know what you're doing, but you'll figure it out." But the inner critic, when you experience IP, isn't that.

Experiencing IP and the intense feelings that follow can cripple you. It's saying statements like "fake it 'til you make it" and beginning to believe you are, in fact, a fake. Your voice convinces your mind and makes you believe you don't have the skills, knowledge, or experience to start a new job, run that business, or write that book.

It is just as important to own your success, to speak kindly to yourself, and use vocabulary that doesn't convince your subconscious you are a fake. Here's how it goes: if you tell yourself you're a fake, you are going to believe it. If you say you are qualified, you will believe it, too. So why not choose the latter? Why not choose to believe in you? You deserve to be exactly where you are right now. You got yourself there. You did it; it's time to say it so you can believe it! Build that internal validation.

I stepped into the clinic room, and Ben was like any other patient. He had recently been diagnosed with head and neck cancer, and I was getting him ready for his radiation and chemotherapy treatment. Ben was seventy-nine years young, dressed in brown slacks and a white button-down corduroy long-sleeve shirt.

He was slightly slumped in the chair, and to my right I noticed his cane leaning against the wall. Ben had arthritis.

From first glance, I expected a talkative person. Most of my senior patients were quite talkative as they didn't have many people to talk to on any given day. Working at a hospital, this was challenging because I found myself often falling behind. Even as a dentist, I sit with my patients and listen to what's going on in their lives and what they may be feeling as they are processing their new cancer diagnosis.

As Ben started telling me a story, I immediately guided him back to the purpose of the visit. I was already running twenty-five minutes behind, and it was only the morning. I could feel my assistant breathing down my neck to try and catch me up.

As I asked Ben questions, he became more direct with his answers. He knew what we needed to get through today, so he participated as any patient would: wide-eyed and concerned, but understanding. Radiation and chemotherapy was going to save his life. I proceeded to describe all of the side effects he would experience and reminded him that I would be with him along the way to answer any questions and support his care during this challenging time.

Head and neck cancer is no walk in the park (not that any cancer is, but side effects do vary). Your mouth becomes sore to the point it feels like it's on fire. You can lose the majority of taste and have difficulty swallowing, which sometimes require a feeding tube. These are only a couple of the symptoms.

I finished examining Ben's mouth, and the appointment was nearly over. I stood up to slowly walk toward the door. This is a sign to both assistant and patient that we are wrapping up the appointment.

"Ben, do you have any questions about anything we talked about today?"

He replied, "Do you think I'll still be able to give presentations while going through radiation?"

I felt my shoulders tighten. Here was this seventy-nine-years-young man who was still giving presentations, and my first thought was, "to whom and why?" As I looked past Ben's shoulder, I could see my assistant glaring at me because she knew exactly what I was going to do.

I pulled the chair back and sat down. "Ben, tell me a little bit more about your presentations, and we can come up with a plan on when and how the radiation will affect you so you can set those presentations up as best as possible."

Ben started to describe to me that he sits on multiple boards. The one that stood out to me was the education board at a veterinary school. His goal was to support the students in their learning endeavors and to provide a location for animals to receive adequate care. My assistant left the room; she knew I was sitting put for a bit.

Ben and I started talking about all of his endeavours, even going back to his early thirties. My memory of this conversation is so vivid that I still get chills down my arms thinking about it.

Ben described to me, "I became CEO overnight at thirty-two. I didn't know what I was doing, and I don't think the board had any confidence in me either. But, the guy before me did a piss-poor job."

I was so intrigued that I kindly asked him if I could pick his brain about the self-doubt he experienced while in the new CEO role.

Ben replied, "I have no other place to be; go for it."

"Did you ever feel like you couldn't do the job?"

"Oh yes, most mornings I woke up thinking, *This will be the day they fire me.*"

"It sounds as if you felt like an impostor in this new role," I said.

"Most definitely. I was in my early thirties and now CEO. I think they expected me to fail. I think I expected me to fail, too."

I asked, "What kept you going back? What helped you break through the self-doubt?"

Slowly, Ben straightened himself in the chair. "I kept showing up." Ben took a pause and then said, "I pushed myself every morning when I got up. I fought back the words I would hear at times. I kept telling myself I will leave here today better than it was yesterday. And I held onto that firmly."

I sat there wide-eyed, absorbing every word.

"Eventually, weeks, months, and years went by. The business grew, people were happy, and I was confident," Ben gleamed.

I looked over at the clock and realized I could spend hours with Ben, but my other patients wouldn't be too happy, so I asked my final question. "Ben, confidence is a finicky thing; it can be fleeting and hard to find at times. What would you tell the person who is a high achiever, but can't believe in their capabilities or can't find their own confidence?"

He grinned and shared, "Life is a book. This, is a chapter. You get to choose when you turn the page, but when you turn that page, you need to write the next page differently than what you wrote today."

I thanked Ben for his time, and he responded, "No, thank you for indulging an old man about his life. I hope you didn't run too far behind."

I immediately ran back to my office and grabbed a Post-it note. I wrote down what Ben had said and decided this was going to be one of my lessons on how to build confidence.

The lesson in what Ben shared with me is: **you get to choose what you write on your page.** You can choose to speak hurtful words to yourself, or you can choose to speak kindly.

By choosing to speak kindly, you are inadvertently building internal validation. *Internal validation* is the proof and positive (or neutral) reinforcement you require to solidify and continue to grow your confidence. It is complimenting yourself, savouring success, and jotting down that time you stepped into your own. Internal validation is stable, consistent, and easily accessible. You are validating who you are and who you have become. It is also reframing what you know your strengths are instead of allowing the outside world to tell you what you should deem a strength.

For example, in today's workplace environment, creative and critical thinking, communication, problem-solving, listening, and showing empathy are considered "soft skills." Tewfik's research showed that people with IP have a grasp on these skills.[16] It is society and culture that have deemed these skills "soft," when in actuality, I would like to reframe and add value to them; these are, in fact, *essential* skills. So go on, embrace them, shout them from the rooftops, and own those skills.

External validation is fleeting, inconsistent, and unreliable. External validation comes from outside sources like compliments from your boss or colleagues, likes on social media, or Google reviews. In my previous examples, I was an external validation to both Anika and my accountability partner. That is why I asked questions and had them reframe so they, too, could build their internal validation. With external validation, you don't know when and if these comments will happen so you constantly search for the next one. Don't get me wrong: if someone compliments you, take note of it and remember, but external validation shouldn't be how you choose to build your confidence.

BRAIN TRAINING EXERCISE: POSITIVE INVESTMENT CONTAINER (PIC FOR SHORT)

This is your piggy bank of internal validation saved for rainy days. A rainy day may be a "crappy feeling" day, a "snide comment from someone" day, or an "I hate the way this outfit looks on me" day. By choosing to write kind words about yourself, you begin to fill the container with moments that bring you joy, happiness, and fulfilment. Ideas of what to put in the container: past achievements, successes, talents, abilities, feelings of accomplishments, feelings of courage or hope, events, days that made you feel content, moments of gratitude, or learned experiences even when they were challenging. You want to put both neutral and positive items into this container. It doesn't have to be all the most amazing stuff you have every done. It can be how you chose to implement a boundary and stick to it to protect your mental space or how you chose to speak kindly on a day that was difficult (more on why neutral is important as well in Part III, Burnout).

When you actively put investments into your piggy bank (your positive investment container), you can pull from the fund on those rainy days. Your container can be physical or digital. It could be a shoe box, a Tupperware container, a journal, or digital photobook. The options are yours to choose.

Over time and without even knowing, your positive investment container will build your confidence. You'll stop thinking of yourself as a fake, and while you soar to new heights, that new inner voice will cheer you on. When you allow your investment to grow, you start to believe your worth. You start to believe you deserve to be right where you are. But most important, you start to believe that you, in fact, are enough.

PART II
PERFECTIONISM

"Be the person that when your feet touch the floor in the morning, the devil says, 'Aww shit . . . they're up.'
—Dwayne "The Rock" Johnson

CHAPTER 5

WHAT IS PERFECTIONISM?

So far you've learned about the five different impostor types: 1. The Perfectionist, 2. The Natural Genius, 3. The Expert, 4. The Lone Wolf, and 5. The Superwoman. Now I'll talk about perfectionism more as a whole, how it fits into the impostor cycle, and how it has a cycle of its own.

I used to pride myself on being a perfectionist, and as previously mentioned I saw myself as the expert and superwoman. At interviews, I explained how being a perfectionist was both a strength and weakness all wrapped up into one. I was smug about it, too. Being a perfectionist meant never being vulnerable or admitting flaws. But that's because I didn't understand what perfectionism is, what it was doing to me, and what it continues to do to high-achieving women. **Perfectionism is self-invented pressure. It sets unrealistic expectations and links our self-worth to the ability to achieve and then keep on achieving.** The definition of perfectionism in the Merriam-Webster dictionary is: "a disposition to regard anything short of perfection as unacceptable."

In psychology, perfectionism is "characterized as striving for flawlessness, setting excessively high standards for performance, and evaluating one's own behaviour overly critically."[17] There are "tendencies to persistently refine and criticize one's own work likely to produce substantial demands and pressures, negatively impacting one's well-being."[18] What's fascinating is I thought I was original by telling employers a weakness of mine was being a perfectionist, but it is a common response for any interviewee across many fields.[19]

Wanting to be perfect comes with many potential negative side effects: chronic stress, habitual worry, stomach ulcers, and sleep disturbances, to name a few. The definition of perfectionism actually includes negative side effects. If we knew the truth about what perfectionism is, would any of us want to be perfect?

The myth I kept telling myself was: Well, I like achieving. I like to work hard, and it motivates me. That's why I demand perfection. It's a true paradox, if you will. I have to keep achieving, because if I don't then I'll feel left out, behind, or I'll never be good enough. I have to keep working hard, because if I take a break then I feel unproductive, which makes me feel guilty. It's the only way I know how to motivate myself, so I keep moving the goal post over the cognitive horizon.

My perfection, success, and happiness were always over the cognitive horizon, and I never actually got there. I compared myself to others. *Will I be the perfect dentist? Will I be the perfect friend? Will I be the perfect partner? Will I be the perfect future mom?* Haven't you ever compared yourself to others, especially to the perfect posts on social media, TV, society, or magazines and wondered: why can't I be like that?

A few years after graduation, I became a full-time staff dentist at a cancer centre, worked as an associate dentist at two other offices, was heavily involved in organized dentistry, and picked up sailing and jiu jitsu as hobbies. I actively dated, trying to find a partner. I even considered freezing an embryo, just in case I didn't find someone. I did my best to take care of my family. I hung out with friends. I was a weekend warrior drinking wine and going out for dinner. Honestly, to an outsider looking in, this seems like I had a pretty great life. Yet, I was only going through the motions. I felt numb.

One day after work, I got off the subway and entered my apartment. As I walked in and closed the door, I gazed past the kitchen into the living room and couldn't take a step forward. My body felt so heavy, and I was drained. I leaned back against the door and, with my jacket still on, slid down until I sat with my knees to my chest. Unable to make dinner, jump in the shower, or do anything, I grabbed my phone and scrolled through social media. Another perfect wedding. Another perfect wedding dress. Another perfect baby shower. Another perfect first home. Another perfect trip. Another perfect smile. Another perfect person. *Ugh, why can't this be you? Why don't you have any of these things?* I couldn't stop scrolling. I needed to see it all. I needed to see everything I was missing and didn't have. I compared myself to people I knew and people I didn't know. Their lives were all put together, and here I was, struggling. Utterly exhausted and tired, I didn't want to feel anything anymore.

An hour or more passed, and I still sat there, scrolling social media. My mind and body were disconnected. I wanted to be perfect so badly that if I couldn't be perfect, then why do anything at all? Being numb was easier. Being numb, to me, meant doing the grind and getting through. I was such a high achiever that I wasn't going to let up and do nothing, but trying to be perfect cost me more than any degree, house, or wedding. The price of perfection was losing *me.*

I worked hard and wanted to be perfect not because I wanted to be successful or have my dreams come true. **I wanted to be perfect because I feared failure and the lack of success.** I feared what I would look like to others and to society. I feared I would let others down, and I feared being alone. But most importantly, I feared the darkness in my mind. That inner voice.

So why do you demand perfection? Perfectionism isn't just about trying to be perfect. Perfectionism is about avoiding mistakes, shame, blame, and judgement . . . to avoid uncertainty.[20] If perfect, then certain. If perfect, then successful. If perfect, then happy. But perfectionism is a perspective. Your perfection and my perfection are not the same. Your success and my success are not the same. Your happiness and my happiness are not the same.

Exploring perfectionism and how it related to IP gave me a better understanding of why high-achieving women put an enormous amount of pressure on themselves that's not healthy or sustainable. **As a reminder, the drive for perfection is a part of the impostor cycle.** Below we are going to explore the pressure you put on yourself by examining your perfectionist rulebook, the perfectionism cycle, and how that fits into experiencing IP.

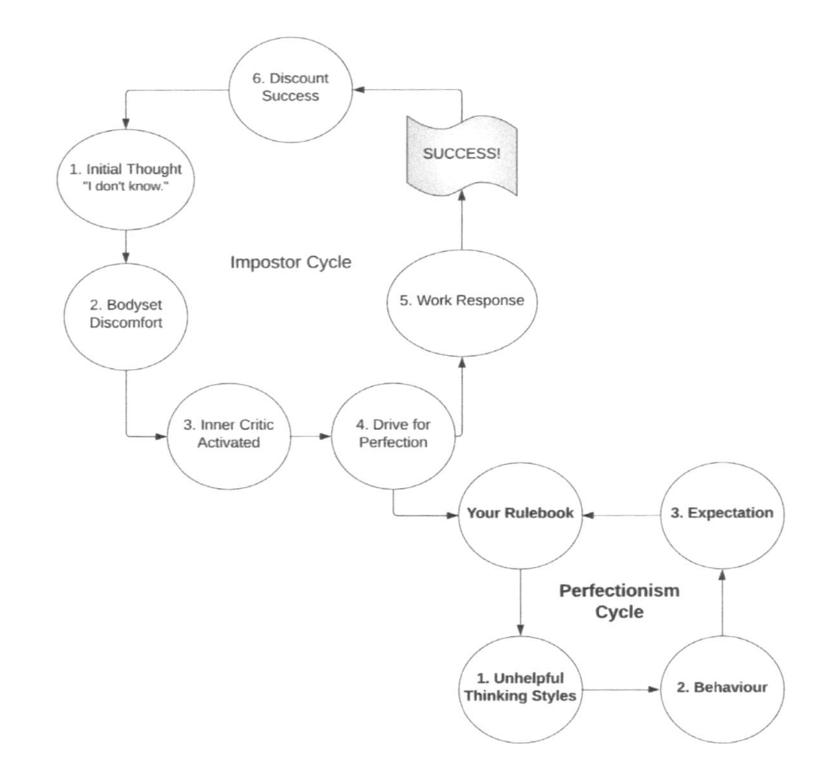

Mind Map: Impostor Cycle + Perfectionism Cycle

CHAPTER 6

YOUR PERFECTIONIST RULEBOOK

We each have a rulebook for ourselves and for the people in our lives. Friend, foe, lover, and family all get a rulebook. We have pages upon pages of how we should live our life and how others should live their lives accordingly in relation to us. Unless you have written it, the rulebook you have is unconscious. It is years in the making, through trial and error. **This rulebook is the map to your success, or should I say, the map to avoid failure.**

The rulebook tells us what we like, what we don't like, how we should behave, experiences we should have, and so on. We've been writing this rulebook our entire life, documenting emotions and experiences that tell us what makes us feel good and what makes us feel bad. The perfectionist portion of the rulebook is a way to set extremely high standards in combination with the ability to be overcritical of ourselves and the outcomes.[21]

The areas in your life that could be impacted depend on your level of striving for perfection. You may set perfectionist standards for work, organization (within your home or office), relationships, social situations (like parties or vacations), or your physical appearance, health, or fitness.

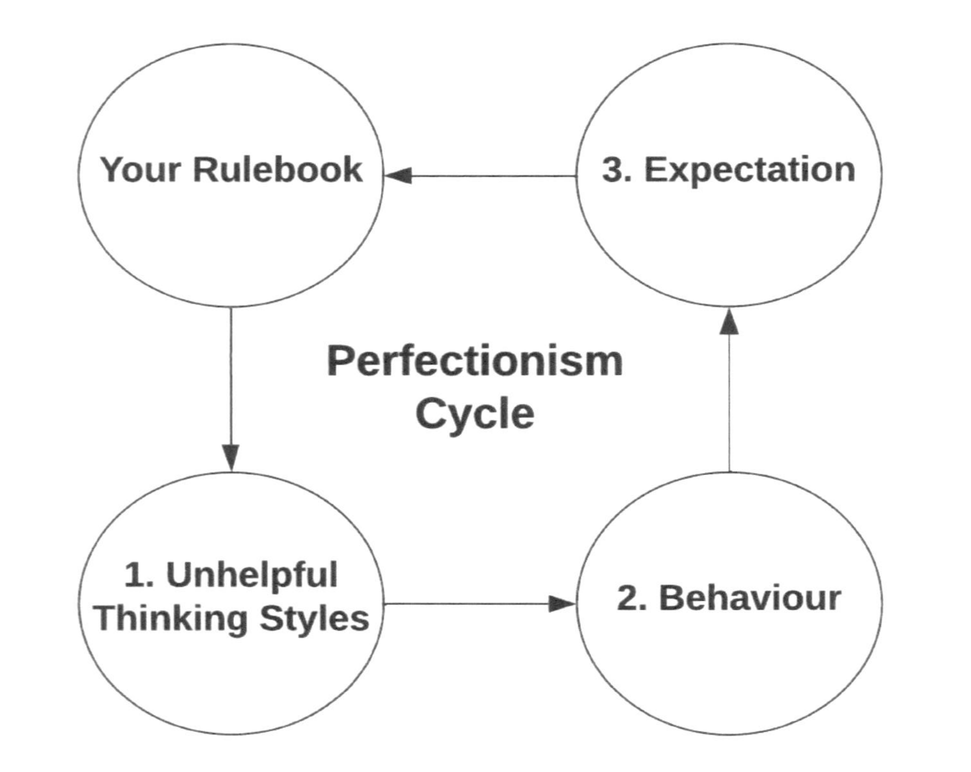

Mind Map: Perfectionism Cycle Simplified

Your rulebook can be broken down into three components: 1. unhelpful thinking styles, 2. behaviours, and 3. expectations. These components allow you to strive for perfection, which keeps you trapped in the perfectionism cycle. I'll go over each in detail, and then I'll show you how to break this cycle.

6.1 UNHELPFUL THINKING STYLES

Unhelpful thinking styles provide a biased perspective of how you see yourself and the world around you. These thoughts and beliefs are unconsciously reinforced over time based on our experiences, good or bad. Because we use them so often, it becomes difficult to recognize when they are featured in our day-to-day thoughts.[22] [23] [24] Any thought can be interpreted negatively, which can prompt an unhelpful thinking style, which then activates your FF response, which also occurs in the impostor cycle. Your attitude and mood can then shift because you feel more nervous or anxious.

There are ten different unhelpful thinking styles we will go over to help you determine which ones you may fall trap to.

1. ALL-OR-NOTHING

This is also known as black-and-white thinking. You may think in terms of extremes, where a project either went absolutely fantastic or horribly awful. There is no in-between.

> **Examples:** I have to show up perfect in all events, tasks, and situations. The expectation is, "All of my work needs to be perfect or I've failed," or "All of my interactions have to be perfect or I screwed it up."

Reframe: I understand there are factors outside of my control. I will try and do my best.

2. OVERGENERALIZING

This unhelpful thinking style has you using words like *every, always, nothing,* or *never.* If, one time, something doesn't go as planned, you interpret it as a future overall pattern. You overgeneralize, thinking nothing will ever go as planned.

Examples: An event doesn't go as planned, and now any future event I host or go to will have the same mishap. An employee doesn't follow through with what I said, so this employee will never follow through. It's saying something like, "Nothing ever works out for me."

Reframe: This event had its challenges, and I can use the information for next time. I will check in with the employee instead of thinking this employee will never follow through.

3. MENTAL FILTER

This unhelpful thinking style is similar to 2. Overgeneralizing; however, it solely focuses on the negatives or failures, thereby excluding any success. It becomes easy to focus only on the negative pieces of information instead of seeing the positives or neutrals as well.

Examples: If I had two bad days in the month of March, then the entire month was seen as bad. If I took months to work on a project and the end result was nearly perfect, I view only the areas I think went wrong. It is easier to say, "I'm a failure" than reflect on any of my successes.

Reframe: If I can choose to filter out the positives, I can also choose to filter out the negatives.

4. MINIMIZING POSITIVE EXPERIENCE

This is similar to 3. Mental Filter. You can see the positives that occurred; however, you reduce any sort of positive experience or achievement because you don't think the positive was truly worth it. You may even think you shouldn't experience the positives because you are only waiting for the other shoe to drop. You disqualify your achievements and reject any form of success.

Examples: A friend praises me, but instead of acknowledging it, it is easier to think, *That friend's comment doesn't count.* Another notorious statement I would hear from both dentists and doctors was, "The only reason I haven't been sued is because I'm nice." There is strong evidence that I am good at what I do, and yet I don't believe it because I reduce the experience.

Reframe: I will accept all comments, even from close friends and family. There is strong evidence I am good at what I do. Period.

5. JUMPING TO CONCLUSIONS

This unhelpful thinking style can be broken down into two types: mind reading and fortune-telling. Mind reading is when you have an incorrect belief that you know what another person is thinking without asking or knowing for certain. Fortune-telling is the tendency to make conclusions or predictions about a situation or person.

Examples: I see a colleague who has an angry expression, and I think they are thinking something negative about me or are mad at me. I even think I'll never find clients who will want to work with me.

Reframe: In reality, I just don't know what they are thinking. Unless I ask them to clarify, there is no reason to interpret the colleague's expression as pertaining to me.

6. SHOULD STATEMENTS

This is where you use statements that include words like *should, ought,* and *must* about yourself or others. If you use these statements about yourself, you can have resulting feelings of guilt and anger toward yourself for not living up to your statements. If you use these statements about others, you can become disappointed they failed to meet your expectations, and this can lead to anger and resentment.

Examples: I should have already been promoted. I must work 24/7 to get ahead.

Reframe: By saying these things, I'm setting myself up for failure before I even begin. It's then easier to say, "I've already failed" before I've even started. I could consider removing *should* from my vocabulary to reset my expectations and remove disappointment before I've even started.

7. CATASTROPHIZING

If this were a sport in the Olympics, I would win a gold medal. Catastrophizing or thinking the worst is when you blow something completely out of proportion. The situation's meaning, importance, or likelihood becomes exaggerated (or extremely minimized).

Example: A very real fear of mine was making a mistake in dentistry. If I made a mistake, then there could be a complication. If there was a complication, then the patient might sue me. If I got sued, I couldn't pay my bills or support my family. I would likely end up homeless and be a total failure in life.

Reframe: Catastrophizing is a way of protecting myself from getting hurt. I used to say "plan for the worst, hope for the best," but planning for the worst meant I never got to enjoy when the best did happen. When a catastrophizing thought presents, I tell myself to go back to the information I already have, and until I know different, I rely on the present information.

8. LABELING

This unhelpful thinking style is the extreme form of 2. Overgeneralizing. It is when you assign preconceived judgements to yourself or others based on one situation.

Example: My favourite is how society has labeled the entire millennial generation as lazy. I used to fight against this stereotype, but I can't argue about the year I was born. I may even go as far as labeling myself by saying, "I'm stupid and I suck at my job." It may be easy to label myself as "stupid" and not think anything of it, but my inner voice is tracking that and going to use it against me in the future.

Reframe: Remove labels and judgements. I could ask myself why I feel the need to label myself negatively.

9. PERSONALIZATION

This unhelpful thinking style blames everything on yourself without logic or reason. Even with evidence proving otherwise, you assume everything is your fault and you take everything personally.

Example: If I have a hard time getting everything on the to-do list done, then I blame myself. I don't take into account if the to-do list was too long, I got a flat tire, and overextended myself. It doesn't matter how hard I try; if something goes wrong, it's always because of me. Someone forgets to take the waste bin out at work, it's my fault. The restaurant gets my order wrong, it's my fault because I likely didn't communicate well enough.

Reframe: I do not need to automatically think something went wrong because of me.

10. EMOTIONAL REASONING

This unhelpful thinking style mixes thoughts and emotions. It is the acceptance of one's emotions as fact. However, feelings are not facts. Just because we feel something doesn't make it true. This is hard for the anxious person because you can confuse intuition with anxiousness (more in Part III, Burnout).

Examples: I feel worthless for stumbling during a presentation and I convince myself I am dumb regardless of how many presentations I've done. A friend is always late. This pisses me off, so I think the friend doesn't care about me or my time. Because I feel a specific way, I convince myself I'm an idiot.

Reframe: I stumbled in a presentation but that doesn't mean I'm dumb. I was able to find my spot and kept going. I will ask my friend why they are late and tell them how I feel.

If you're looking for more tips and techniques to help navigate each unhelpful thinking style, check out my online book portal, www.speakkindlyyourelistening.com.

All of these unhelpful thinking styles are ill-natured perspectives of how you choose to see yourself. They allow you to speak negatively toward yourself, and by listening to what you say, you begin to believe it.

Jamie is a doctor and a client of mine. She owns her own clinic, and her hobbies include surfing and painting.

Her painting mentors are, as she describes, grumpy old men. These mentors tell her to look to social media for praise because they aren't going to give it to her. Jamie has always had a hard time beholding her work. We, as high achievers, can be our own worst critics. However, if you continue to shit-talk your own work or belittle yourself, then you will believe it. How can you become the artist, the mom, or the athlete you want to be if you beat yourself up?

Jamie's assistant asked her to put up her work in the office one day. Jamie was completely opposed to this idea until her assistant wore her down. She brought in a bunch of her artwork and told her assistant to hang up whatever she wanted.

Not even a day later, Jamie walked through her office, her eyes wide. "You chose all my horrible paintings except for one."

That one painting Jamie loved hung at the front for all to see. Jamie had spent hours on this piece, as she usually does when she paints scenery and landscapes. The painting was full of fine details, from the brushstrokes to the paint colours. Jamie loved the final product. As she turned the corner, the next piece caused her mouth to drop.

Absolutely horrified, Jamie said to Miranda, "Why did you put *that* one up?"

Miranda grinned. "*I* like it."

Jamie hated it.

Jamie told me that painting was a challenge from her mentor. It was never supposed to see the light of day, and yet there it was, hanging in the clinic for all to see. Jamie had to walk past this painting every day, multiple times a day.

In that moment, Jamie sighed. "Just take it down and pick another one."

"No, I like it."

That's where Jamie and I went to work on challenging her unhelpful thinking styles and learning to embrace imperfection by changing her narrative. To start, Jamie described her painting as an incomplete thought.

I asked, "Why don't you like it?"

"It was the end of the palette and I only spent seven minutes on it."

"If you had a full palette, would it have mattered?"

"No."

"If you spent more than seven minutes on it, would it have mattered?"

"Yes."

"What would have changed?"

"The brushstrokes would have been more complete."

"If you spent ten hours on it, would you feel different?"

"Yes."

"Would ten hours have been enough?"

"Sometimes."

"Have there been times even when you spent ten hours that you didn't like a piece?"

"Yes."

"Does the time really matter?"

Jamie thought for a moment and then said, "I guess not."

"This was a different challenge and a different style of doing your artwork."

"Totally."

"Can you believe that even if you don't like it, someone else would?"

"Maybe."

Maybe was all I needed for Jamie to start to shift her perspective.

Our conversation continued when I said, "And what's that saying about artwork or creativity?"

"It's in the eye of the beholder," Jamie reminded herself.

"Can you imagine that someone falls deeply in love with that piece and each day they wake up every morning grateful to have seen that work of art?"

"I can."

"Can you believe in that piece even if you don't like it?"

"I can try . . ."

That is all I ask of my clients: to try to see a different perspective by changing their narrative.

I end all my sessions with a recap of what we talked about. I teach them to ask themselves different questions instead of feeling stuck thinking: "Why do I suck at this? Why can't I ever be good at this?"

At the end of Jamie's session, I could hear her tone change. I could hear the spirit in her voice being lifted. I could hear the smile through a shift in her tone and energy, especially when I cheered, "You know you own an art gallery, right? You own both a clinic and an art gallery."

Jamie was shocked because it was true. "Oh my God, I do own an art gallery!"

It may not be the conventional art gallery, but it's still an art gallery nonetheless. It is all in how you choose to view the situation, event, or obstacle. It's in the words you choose and how that perspective changes.

In this example, Jamie was experiencing 3. Mental Filter, 5. Jumping to Conclusions, 6. Should Statements, and 10. Emotional Reasoning. She filtered her past experiences that allowed her to create a painting in seven minutes. Years of hard work allowed her to not just start but also finish the painting with vibrant, deep colours. She jumped to the conclusion that no one else would or could ever like this because she didn't approve of it. Her Should Statements caused her to experience anger and frustration with her own capabilities. Lastly, she linked how she *felt* with what the artwork must *be*. I had Jamie send me all her paintings; I looked through them and then asked her which one she disliked. It was the one I liked the most. Those vibrant, deep colours are the colours I enjoy in this world. I bought Jamie's painting and proudly hang it in my office to this day.

Altering your unhelpful thinking style takes time and practice. In Part I, we talked about creating self-awareness. This holds true here as well. You're not going to stop the unhelpful thinking style immediately. But, we can put parameters in place to intervene in the moment.

BRAIN TRAINING EXERCISE: THOUGHT ANESTHETIZED

The following exercise is to be used when your thoughts are starting to turn negative in a new or stressful situation, like when you are getting ready to perform, are in the middle of a procedure, or are starting a new job. The goal is to stop the unhelpful thinking style that occurs while you are in the midst of doing something important.

As a reminder from the impostor cycle, your initial thought activates your FF response that, in turn, awakens your inner critic to spew unkind words. Here, your inner critic may use one of the unhelpful thinking styles to create negative self-talk, keeping your FF response turned on, spiking your adrenaline, and impinging on how you perform the task at hand. When there is too much adrenaline, your thoughts can be chaotic and disorganized, affecting your problem-solving and decision-making abilities.

Getting back to the brain training exercise, we are going to put the thought to sleep, to anesthetize it. This is a great way to think of it, because we aren't suppressing or pushing away our thoughts and emotions, but putting them on hold for a time and place where we feel safe to explore them. Amongst the feelings of chaos or disruption, you can still choose calmness and composure.

Example: Let's say you are getting ready to start a new job, and, minutes before you go, you tell yourself, "You suck and someone else should be doing this." This is where you tell yourself to STOP. Pack it away for later. Ask yourself, "Is this thought helping me solve the problem?" If the answer is "no," then move on. You can also repeat a mantra that reminds you that you are safe to help ease your FF response activated in that moment—something along the lines of: "I will take one step, then another," or "This is the moment I choose to think different," or "I feel my butterflies but it doesn't mean I can't." At the end of the day, give yourself permission to bring the thought you anesthetized back to the present moment and ask yourself, "Why did I think that, and what was I worried about?"

Then, put a worry time on it. Set a timer for a specific amount of time, your choice. It could be five, ten, or thirty minutes. Allow your brain to run through every possible unhelpful thought. Allow it to catastrophize, allow it to overgeneralize, allow it to emotionally reason. If that's where the thoughts want to go, let them. Give your brain permission to think, because it is doing exactly what it knows how to do: to think.

At the end of the worry time, set yourself a one-minute timer. This is where you will put the initial thought in its place. Remind your brain of past evidence that you are capable. Repeat a mantra, like: "I'm capable and willing to learn." If you want to use the same mantra from before, then do it. If at this point you want to adjust, do it. Find what works specifically for you. You can even go over how your first day at your new job went. As a reminder from 3.6 Discounting Success in chapter three, this is the difference between reflection and rumination. Reflection allows you to grow and improve; rumination slowly destroys your confidence.

By creating a worry time and a safe space to reflect afterwards, you begin to deactivate your FF response and, in turn, create a new way of thinking and a new neural network that actives your parasympathetic nervous system. This is also known as the "rest-and-digest" response (more on this in Part III, Burnout).

By creating a new neural network, you give yourself the opportunity to take a different path whenever you experience an unhelpful thinking style. The above unhelpful thinking styles are self-invented pressures of unrealistic expectations that create a rulebook that forces you to be "perfect" and unable to make mistakes. How can you be perfect when life comes with uncertainties? It should be enough to say, "I am prepared and will figure the mess out when it happens, if it even does." It's okay to not know, and it's okay to embrace the unknown.

It is easy to condemn ourselves when we look back and think "Well, I could have . . ." or "If only I had known . . ." but that is a form of reflection. Once you *do* know, you think and do different. Hindsight will always be 20/20 because you now have experience and more knowledge. Don't allow that inner critic to discount your newly obtained knowledge by disregarding your success and keeping you stuck in the past.

When you change your unhelpful thinking style, you change what you hear, and you change your inner voice.

6.2 BEHAVIOURS

So far, I have discussed how the unhelpful thinking styles can be used by your inner critic to put an enormous amount of pressure on you to be "perfect." Now, we are going to bring together how they both influence our daily behaviours. To feel safe and in control, striving for perfection and acting subconsciously or consciously toward perfection provide our mind with certainty. This could be as simple as creating a grocery list, checking it a few times, then deciding to leave the house. Each time we commit to a behaviour for the purpose of striving for perfection, we step into the next component of the perfectionism cycle. This provides necessary feedback to our subconscious mind; confirmation that what we are doing will help us reach perfection. That information allows us to create an environment that is both predictable and controllable, even though we all know everything is not within our control. When we feel like our job or home life are floundering, we as high achievers turn inwards to control what we can: our behaviour.

Perfectionist behaviours are deliberate actions or habits that exist to reduce anxiety of feared or uncertain situations.[25] When used, these behaviours act as a temporary relief from worry and stress, as they reduce your FF response for a short period of time.

Despite the short-term benefits, these behaviours can stifle your overall growth by not giving you the opportunity to explore mistakes or gain awareness about your ability to cope with failure. They are a protective mechanism to avoid feeling sad, ashamed, or disappointed with yourself. These behaviours deplete energy and come at a cost, also robbing you of your time, as if you are paying a toll for trying to be perfect. Types of perfectionist behaviours include: over-preparing, excessive checking, redoing, excessive organizing and list making, reassurance seeking (from others), lack of delegating, and micromanaging. I go over these in more depth in the table below.

COMMON PERFECTIONIST BEHAVIOURS

Behaviour	What is it?	Example
Over-preparing	Anticipating every possible thing that could go wrong, and still being afraid you haven't prepared enough.	Running a meeting and trying to think of every question that might be asked. You continue to stress because you think you didn't prepare enough.

Behaviour	What is it?	Example
Excessive Checking	Going over your work or someone else's work multiple times.	You're getting ready to hand in a report. You've edited it numerous times. You can't hand it in early because you have to check it right up to the deadline.
Redoing	Whether you or someone else has completed the task, if it isn't to your level of perfection, you will likely redo it.	You task an employee to send email invites to your clients. You don't like the proof and instead of offering suggestions to change, you redo the whole thing yourself.
Excessive Organizing and List Making	Before getting started on a task, you feel the need to organize or make lists. Most times after making the list or organizing, you're too tired to actually do the task.	Having to clean a space before you get anything started. Creating list after list but not feeling like you're crossing anything off.
Reassurance Seeking	Reaching out to others for confidence instead of believing your own words.	Messaging your boss asking if you have done everything right because you fear being fired.

Behaviour	What is it?	Example
Lack of Delegating	Doing everything on your own or saying "yes" when you could get help from others.	A project comes up and instead of delegating tasks, you decide to do the whole project on your own.
Micromanaging	Watching every little detail in others. This removes autonomy, and employees lose trust in their own capabilities.	You expect your team to run every question, concern, or new idea by you. Team members lose trust in themselves and don't feel they are capable of making own decisions. This gives them the opportunity to hound you while on vacation or at home.

For me, that drive for perfection came at the cost of lost energy and time. I was over-preparing, micromanaging, refusing to delegate and needing reassurance from the people around me, only to feel temporarily reassured from worry. The price of perfection was losing me and my inner cheerleader. Being the first to arrive and the last to leave work allowed more time for me to scrutinize all I said and did wrong throughout the day. Micromanaging my employees didn't make me a better leader. In fact, it crippled my team's autonomy. I thought asking for help meant I couldn't figure it out on my own, which left me feeling inadequate and embarrassed. Work was never left at work, because I would text colleagues and friends when I got home, asking for reassurance that I did everything right and that I was good enough.

Other people's opinions of me, whether good or bad, overshadowed my inner cheerleader and allowed my inner critic to shout at me. If someone criticized me, my inner critic berated me harshly, while if someone complimented me, the reassurance was so fleeting that I never had time to process the compliment. I no longer believed I was doing well at work, that I was a good friend, or that I was worthy. My happiness and confidence depended on others' perceptions of me, so my inner cheerleader became quiet and neglected. Each day those perfectionist behaviours dominated was another day my confidence was ripped to shreds. Not only that, but those unhelpful thinking styles and behaviours stole my time and energy.

Before Rey and I started working together she was stuck hating her job and feeling exhausted at the end of the day. She told me, "If something isn't done right at work, I end up redoing it. So when problems come up, I just take care of it because then I know it'll get done perfectly."

I see this often in many of my clients who are high achievers and perfectionists. It is easier to control results if you, the high achiever, does it all, but this also means you are exhausted, overwhelmed, and frustrated.

Over the course of a few months, Rey and I worked on delegating tasks and teaching others in order to get desired outcomes. I had Rey start small. On a day when her colleague called in sick to work, she usually would jump into action and pick up all the slack. Instead, she started asking for others to step in as she delegated tasks to be completed.

My favourite way to coach delegation and reduce redoing tasks is to show them that it takes the equivalent amount of time to do it themselves as it does to teach. When you help others improve their skill set, they build confidence to figure things out on their own long term, as well as complete tasks to your level of expectation. But you have to give them the opportunity to grow, and that starts with learning to delegate and teach.

Before, when Rey's team members were finished setting up for an event, she would go back through and adjust to her liking. Now, Rey outlines what her expectations are to the team and supports their decisions. She began to build confidence in her team and in her ability to delegate to the appropriate team members. She noticed her team became more creative and confident, and she sparingly redid tasks. Instead, she continued to use each of those opportunities to build her team's skills and because of this, she had more time and energy for projects that required her strengths. As she stepped into her strengths, she noticed her inner voice changing its tone. It no longer got hung up on perfectionist behaviours. As Rey noticed her energy return, her emotions didn't feel out of control, and she began to witness successes in her day to day, thereby building her confidence one step at a time and restoring her energy. She stopped calling herself a perfectionist and didn't feel like she was being run ragged. Rey slowly learned how to change her inner critic to inner cheerleader because she now knew her unhelpful thinking patterns and behaviours that kept her stuck.

TIPS FOR PERFECTIONIST BEHAVIOURS

Behaviour	Try This
Over-preparing	Set an allotted amount of time that you will prepare. Stick to it. When you have finished preparing (even if it is in a shorter period of time), step away and say, "I have prepared."

Behaviour	Try This
Excessive Checking	Allow yourself to check something only once. Commit to memory that you have checked it and are assured it is the correct information. You can even say it out loud to activate more of your senses to commit it further to memory.
Redoing	If something isn't perfect, try to see a different perspective or give the task back to the individual to improve. Do not take it on yourself. Instead, offer suggestions on what needs to be improved and use it as a teaching experience. If you completed the task, ask yourself, "Would redoing really benefit that much more?"
List Making and Excessive Organizing	Write out a shorter list of things to do. You will feel more accomplished when it is done instead of writing a never-ending list that never gets accomplished. If you do have a long list of things to do, stop just getting through them, and try to enjoy why they are on the list to begin with. For example, if you are going grocery shopping, it's not that you *have* to go, it's because you want to nourish yourself. For organizing, try to leave something out of place that you wouldn't usually leave out of place. Assess what happens. Does someone else pick up the slack? Are you able to focus on other things?
Reassurance Seeking	When you are about to pick up your phone and text your friend for reassurance, ask yourself what you are currently doubting about yourself. Then, find a tangible answer you believe your friend would say. Repeat your answer to yourself.

Behaviour	Try This
Lack of Delegating	Start small by delegating tasks that will get short-term results. That way you can assess the results and see how delegating is going. Sometimes you may have to adjust what gets delegated based on the other person's strengths. You can only learn what those strengths are by giving tasks to these individuals, including your kids, your partner, and colleagues.
Micromanaging	Trust in your team (family, friends, and colleagues). Give individuals autonomy to make their own mistakes. Trust that you have shown you are there to play a supportive role even when they make a decision. Lean on past evidence, even if small, that they, too, will make the right decision for this moment. When the moment passes, you can then reassess and determine if a teaching moment is needed, or you can commit to memory that this individual is in fact capable.

Getting stuck in the perfectionism cycle can be reinforced by the behaviours which turn into crutches of temporary relief. No one is born with 100 percent confidence; it is built over time by recognizing your abilities in both success and failure. However, you have to reflect on your struggle with both success and failure. If you only focus on the failure, you reinforce specific perfectionist behaviours and you can't build your confidence.

When you stop over-preparing and excessively checking, you realize you don't have to have everything perfect and you'll still be enough—actually, more than enough: ample and abundant. When you stop redoing things and making lists, you start to build your trust in others and you believe what you have finished is in fact good. When you stop seeking reassurance from others, you give your inner voice the opportunity to speak up and you only have to listen. **By interrupting perfectionist behaviours, you will soon come to realize the way you have been doing things doesn't have to be the only way.**

6.3 EXPECTATIONS

We are still making our way around the perfectionism cycle, and the next component after unhelpful thinking styles and behaviours is setting expectations. If you claim yourself as being a perfectionist, the expectations you set for yourself can be excessively high. They are self-invented and created over time as a checkpoint to determine your success and happiness. As you keep achieving and moving through life, these expectations continue to be adjusted based on the happiness and success you seek. Back in Part I, I mentioned if you move the goal post too fast without acknowledging your accomplishments, your success and happiness are always out of reach, over the cognitive horizon. When you decide to set a goal, you set expectations for those goals. As the goals shift, your expectations get adjusted based on the goal you are achieving, and expectations are linked to your behaviours and thinking styles, which operate subconsciously on auto-pilot.

Take for example, your morning routine. The alarm rings and you jet forward to start brewing coffee. While you wait, you head to the bathroom to wash your face and put on make-up. Your routine is going as planned so you head back to grab the cup of coffee and walk to the bedroom to get changed. Getting ready to leave the house, you pass through the hallways, grab your keys, lock the door, walk to the car, start the engine, and drive to work. Your morning routine is on autopilot and the day-to-day actions have been hardwired in your brain to ease decision-making and prevent decision fatigue.

Depending on your expectations around people, work, habits, and experiences, being a perfectionist demands a high outcome of feeling satisfied. The coffee had *better* taste good, the keys had *better* be in their spot, the car had *better* start without a problem, and you had *better* arrive to work without someone cutting you off. When your needs are met and expectations satisfied, you feel more in control of your environment and that contributes to having a "good day," and feeling happy, successful, optimistic, hopeful, and fulfilled. All of these positive or neutral emotions start to add up, and your inner cheerleader can use these moments to grow your confidence.

For the perfectionist, the expectations you have for yourself and others can be high, inflexible, and unrealistic, allowing no room for disruption or growth. Most unrealistic expectations are unlikely to be met and come at a considerable cost, whether that is time, energy, money, or even relationships. You may use expectations as forms of evaluations for others and yourself. Yet, these evaluations are biased and skewed since your inner critic has criticized you for some time now. Many of the impostor and perfectionist rules you have written in your rulebook are inaccurate and a bunch of bullshit. You read that right, and I'm here to tell you, as a friend, coach, and your cheerleader, those perceived rules you have written about yourself can be rewritten and changed. Here's the cherry on top: you have likely written a rulebook for others to follow as well, yet you haven't given them a copy. When they don't meet your expectations, you can get angry at them, but they never knew what those expectations were in the first place. Not only is this exhausting but it puts a strain on the relationships you have with others and with yourself.

At the age of twenty-nine, I began to lecture to other departments at my cancer centre about the oral side effects post–radiation therapy for head and neck cancer patients. When the chief of dentistry at the new hospital asked me to participate, he said a twenty-minute seminar would suffice. I spent *months* working on this seminar. The slide deck had to be perfect, the visuals had to be perfect, my tone of voice and stance had to be perfect. This was going to be one of the first times I lectured on this topic, and I wasn't going to allow for any mistakes to condemn my future goal of becoming chief of dentistry, nor did I want to look like a fool. It was days leading up to the event when the chief of dentistry wandered into my office and sat down. "How's the presentation coming along?"

I flashed a grin, hoping to hide my anxiousness and fear. "It's great, thanks."

He asked delicately, "Can you pull it up and go over it with me?"

My grin dropped and I hesitated. "Sure."

It was already open on my computer. My hand was shaky as I clicked through the presentation. I thoughtfully vocalized the information and research that would be shared with the audience.

He sat carefully thinking, and after what felt like an eternity, he spoke. "Don't be anxious. You know more than anyone in that room about this specific topic."

He was right. In this situation, I was the only dentist in the room among nurses, radiation techs, physiotherapists, medical and radiation oncologists, head and neck surgeons, speech language pathologists, and medical students. Each one of those individuals who sat in the room with me was knowledgeable about *their* specific areas.

I had forgotten that not only did I have a specific knowledge about dental effects for the cancer patient, but I had a degree in dentistry, which came with many years of education and experience. I needed a reminder that I am an expert in my field.

As perfectionists, there are times where we forget past evidence and set high expectations for ourselves because the fear of failure, the fear of making a mistake, and the fear of disapproval outweigh experience, knowledge, skill set, and abilities. As I reflect back on this first presentation, two key points at that time stand out to me:

1. How I kept myself stuck in the perfectionist cycle
    - Expectation: *All* my presentations moving forward would take *months* to put together.
    - Thinking style: All-Or-Nothing.
    - Feeling: Prevent embarrassment
    - Behaviours: Over-Preparing and Excessive Checking
2. How I got myself out of the perfectionist cycle
    - Expectation: I may not know everything, but I do know a lot about specific topics and should lean on that information (the words shared by the chief of dentistry).
    - Thinking Style: Open-minded and using past evidence
    - Feeling: Satisfied
    - Behaviour: Not spending enormous amounts of time getting stuck researching information and reminding myself of information I already know as well.

Expectations are constantly being rewritten in your rulebook as you accomplish your goals and successes. It is just as much a priority to reflect on what went well as it is to figure out what didn't go well. You can break down each component and focus on the information it provided you to create future success. If you only ruminate and focus on what didn't go well, without looking to improve, then you keep yourself stuck, and you don't give yourself the opportunity to speak kindly to yourself. **Learning to set realistic and healthy expectations allows your inner voice to congratulate yourself and remind you of your true potential.** It's another step to building your confidence and believing in yourself.

Evie sets extremely high and unrealistic expectations for herself. She became a client of mine by stumbling on my social media page, and we started working together when she began a new job with more responsibility. She stayed late and arrived early but still felt inadequate and ashamed. She thought that by this time at the new job, she should be more productive and able to take on additional leadership roles.

She compared herself to others at the company. "Why is this taking me forever? I should already know this."

Evie struggled not because she didn't know what she was doing, but because it was a new environment with new people and new systems to learn. Her expectations were set so high that she couldn't see how far she had already come and the qualifications she already had. She even had evidence communicated to her in her early performance review that she was exactly where she needed to be. Evie stared at the evidence in front of her and yet she couldn't internalize her skills because she had stepped into using her unhelpful thinking styles: a negative mental filter and minimizing her positive past experiences.

Evie scoffed, "They are only saying that to be nice. It's only a matter of time before they fire me."

Evie had never been fired from a previous job, yet she wholeheartedly believed that was going to happen. She thought the worst of herself, minimized the positives, excessively prepared, and overworked.

On one of our calls I asked, "What would make you believe you are doing well at your new job?"

She replied bluntly, "Having years of experience."

It was time to shift Evie's perspective. "Let's say you have years of experience. What specifically would make you feel confident?"

Evie thought for a moment. "Knowing I have projects that have been successful."

"Do you have projects from your last job that were successful?"

"Of course."

"So would you say you have years of experience?"

She hesitated, and then lowered her voice. "It doesn't count," she said slowly.

"Why doesn't it count?" I contended.

"Because that was at a different job and I need to prove myself again."

This is a usual sentiment I find from high achievers, thinking they have to prove themselves time and time again, and not recognizing that all of their skills, successes, credentials, and knowledge are completely transferable. The only difference: time, location, and people.

"Evie, do you think you showed your abilities and that's why you were hired?" I didn't skip a beat or let her answer. "Because if your new employer didn't think you were a good fit, they either wouldn't have hired you and they likely would have provided you with ways to improve at your performance review."

There was silence on the call, and I knew Evie was pondering. I continued, "Tell me about one of your past projects."

For the next ten minutes, Evie explained to me in detail about the previous projects that were successful and why they were successful. She shared team wins and personal wins along with the shortcomings and how she had improved for the subsequent projects. She described to me her experience and growth over many years.

I finally asked, "Do you have years of experience, yes or no?"

Evie took a deep breath, "Yes, but . . ."

Immediately I jumped in, "No buts. Focus on what we just spoke about. Those memories are evidence that sets the stage for you to reset your inner voice by changing the unhelpful thinking style, behaviour, and expectation."

Evie had all of the experience she needed; I only needed to remind her because she had forgotten about the concrete evidence. The difference at her new job was not her capabilities but the uncertainty around something new, so I reminded Evie of one thing that was both constant and certain. Herself.

As we wrapped up our phone conversation, Evie asked, "Do you think I can start to go in at regular hours?"

"What do you think?"

"Yeah, I'm going to try sticking to set work hours so I have time for me again."

Evie started to practice setting healthy expectations for herself, and you can do the same.

BRAIN TRAINING EXERCISE: RESETTING EXPECTATIONS

When checking in to see if you are setting an unrealistic or realistic expectation, ask yourself these three questions:

1. Is my expectation realistic and attainable? It has to be achievable without feeling like you are compromising your being or selling your soul.
2. Is my expectation rigid or flexible? This allows you to focus on the progress and not the end result. You make room for exceptions so you can modify your expectations when necessary.
3. Is my expectation worth the cost? The cost is your time and energy. If it isn't worth giving up your finite time and energy, you will want to reconsider.

PROCESSING UNREALISTIC EXPECTATIONS

Unrealistic Expectation	The Thought	Reframe to Healthy Expectation	Actional Step
I am not done working unless it is perfect.	Judges self harshly and never lives up to expectation.	I am done working after a set amount of time; then I will take a break.	Set time blocks. Stick to them. Schedule breaks.
I don't want to disappoint anyone.	Cares so much that loses self when making everyone else happy.	I will do my best, and it is not my responsibility to make everyone happy.	Avoid personalizing other people's reactions. Take responsibility for your own happiness.
I should be further ahead.	Frustrated and disappointed with self by comparing self to others.	I am exactly where I need to be. I will get to where I want to go in time.	Stop comparing yourself to others. Reflect on your past steps and why you want to keep pushing yourself.

You can build your own table with the same boldface title. Fill in your experiences with unrealistic expectations and the thoughts that came with them. Then ask yourself how you would reframe each one, and create action steps. You can also find an empty table to fill in on the book portal, www.speakkindlyyourelistening.com.

CHAPTER 7

STRIVING FOR PERFECTION —THE HARSH REALITY

Up until now, I have shown you that your drive for perfection has been reinforced by the rulebook you have created over many years. **Unhelpful thinking styles, the behaviours that follow, and the unrealistic expectations combine to form your inner voice, your inner critic.** At the beginning of Part II, I shared the perfectionism cycle; however, it can be broken down even further. Below is a more complex and detailed version of the perfectionism cycle and why it continues to persist.

Let me now walk you through the expanded version, because experiencing perfectionism isn't as simple as the original version. When your inner critic makes itself known, it can use the combination of unhelpful thinking styles and perfectionist behaviours to set unrealistic expectations. So the drive for perfection puts an enormous amount of pressure on you, including how you choose to speak to yourself. If you fail to meet those unrealistic expectations, then you give your inner critic the license to criticize yourself and write new pages in your perfectionist rulebook. Think of it as your inner critic picking up a pen and paper, and scribbling another subsection about why you are and will never be good enough.

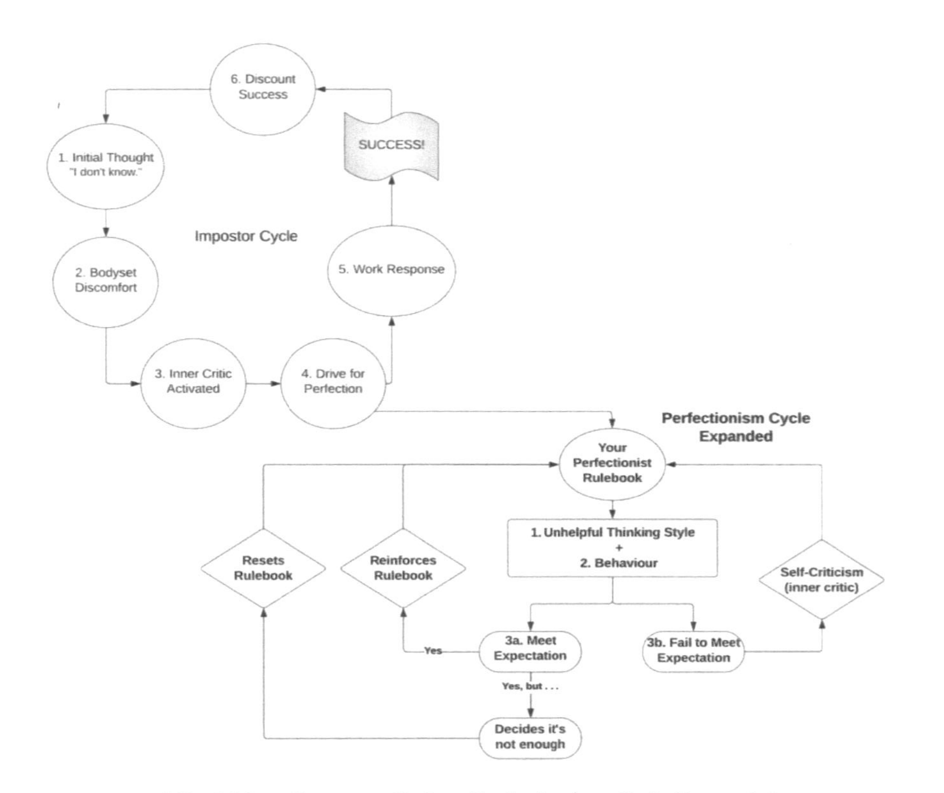

Mind Map: Impostor Cycle + Perfectionism Cycle Expanded

If your expectations are met, the information reinforces your perfectionist rulebook and you continue to use your already existing unhelpful thinking styles and behaviours as motivators. If you met your expectations but decided they weren't high enough, then you reset the expectations in your rulebook and never live up to the new expectations or step into your success. It feels like a lose-lose, "damned if you do and damned if you don't" kind of situation. Time and time again, cycle after cycle, your critic reminds you that you're never enough, and your confidence remains fleeting. No matter the experience, being a perfectionist constantly provides inaccurate self-evaluations and makes you question your overall worth.

I am here to show you that by altering your inner voice, reframing your thoughts and thinking styles, trying new behaviours, and setting realistic expectations, you will come to learn that you are always enough and you have been enough this entire time. It's hard to accept, but somewhere along the way, you stopped believing in yourself.

PERFECTIONISM AND THE INTOLERANCE FOR UNCERTAINTY

When I first started coaching, I received a private message through one of my social media accounts. This is what it said:

Jessica,

I thought that I was an emotionally stable person. I was a happy person and I wasn't anxious at work, even though stressful. I found everything in my life to be very difficult. My employer received a complaint from a disgruntled customer about my attitude. This all happened within the first month of a new job. I had never received a complaint before and previous employers and colleagues have always complimented my cheerfulness.

I started getting panic attacks. My drive to work was almost an hour and my hands were sweaty and I had heart palpations. I couldn't sleep at night and I always felt exhausted.

Even after the complaint was dealt with, I never felt like going to work but I was always working. I worked harder than I have ever worked before. But, none of that mattered. Things were never perfect enough...I was never good enough. I knew something needed to change because I couldn't keep living like this.

When I read this message, I thought I was reading a letter I had written to myself. This was exactly what I had gone through, including the complaint. Telling myself repeatedly that "I was fine and that I should be able to suck it up" got me by (for a while). People around me kept saying, "Don't worry, it'll get better," so I waited and hoped for a change to click into place where I would be perfect, successful, and happy.

That was 100 percent wrong because trying to be perfect all the time meant battling the qualms of uncertainty. This message isn't the only message I have received like this. I get these messages far too often. Women reach out to me sharing their story but not knowing where to start, feeling overwhelmed and stuck. **The deep desire I hear from women is, "I want to be happier and less stressed."**

A resounding reason of why you feel stuck are the endless questions of what-ifs . . . What if I'm not smart enough? What if I'm not pretty enough? What if I'm not good with my money? What if I make the wrong decision? What if, what if, what if. The what-ifs aren't actually helping when you aren't answering the questions. Indeed, the lack of answers makes you anxious about the future and depressed about the past. You become paralyzed because the intolerance of uncertainty and wanting to be perfect are linked to worry and anxiety.[26] The more control we feel we have over outcomes and our environment, the less anxious, angry, and sad we are.[27] The more we assume and convince ourselves we are failures, the more anxious, angry, resentful, and frustrated we become. Being a perfectionist is not just about avoiding mistakes, but controlling how we see ourselves and how we think others perceive us. If we revisit the what-if questions, they sound a lot like fear—fear of a mistake, fear of imperfection, fear of failure, fear of disapproval, and the fear of uncertainty.

What happens when you mix the fear of uncertainty with someone who experiences perfectionism? You get a high achiever who never lives up to her potential and never believes in her abilities. You get a woman who stays stuck—stuck in a shitty job, stuck in a shitty house, stuck in a shitty relationship, just stuck. **Perfectionism and an intolerance for uncertainty mean you think mistakes or imperfections will lead to negative outcomes, which will be absolutely catastrophic.** This means you think you'll be unable to cope with the negative outcomes, and it will reflect on who you are as a high achiever. Being a perfectionist can cause social isolation, performance anxiety, limited interests, and decreased confidence. Speaking unkindly to yourself may have been useful to be "perfect," but it has a lasting effect on your mood where you generally feel low about yourself.

This thought process all happens so fast subconsciously that it becomes easier to stay where you are instead of answering the what-ifs and accepting uncertainty as a part of life. A perfectionist strives for perfection to obtain certainty, to feel like they are in control. If they control the outcome, then they control how they think and feel. Perfectionists want to feel "successful."

Brené Brown, in *Atlas of the Heart,* describes the emotion of surprise as a conduit between two other emotions: the one before the surprise and the one after. Surprise itself lasts only a couple of seconds. While on a hike, I listened to her book and halted in my tracks because it connected the pieces for me on why perfectionists don't like surprises; they can't control the outcome and fear what they could potentially feel or think about themselves. But here's the truth: when my inner critic was at its worst, I was unaware that the one thing I could control was my voice.

The perfectionism cycle exists because there are many short-term positives: it is socially accepted to be a perfectionist, it provides structure and control, it allows you to avoid failures, and it does bring achievements. However, the costs often outweigh the positives, as being a perfectionist uses enormous amounts of time and energy. Real talk: two items are finite and limited in this world, and once they are gone, you can't get them back, and they are: time and energy.

A friend of mine messaged me in a panic one day:

> *I think I need it to be perfect right now. I need to know that my work and effort will be perfect. I know my mindset is: I need it to be perfection. So, I begin to doubt if I was doing it right or if I did something wrong. I constantly think I'm the one to blame if something goes wrong. Then I doubt my skills and question my capabilities but I also know I need to grow. And then I get right back to thinking, I need it to be perfect right now. It's a fucking cycle.*

Going around this cycle like you are on a merry-go-round is exhausting. It feels like it's never-ending. Many high achievers believe perfectionism allows you to be efficient, organized, and prepared. Do not mistake this as the pursuit of excellence, because perfectionism is a paradox. Perfectionist thinking, behaviours, and expectations don't actually make you perfect. Instead, they make you feel frustrated, upset, stressed, and exhausted with yourself and others. If you choose to break the cycle, you, too, can change your inner voice and build your confidence. It is your responsibility to take care of you and your voice. It really is that simple—time to alter your inner narrative and have an impact on your perfectionism cycle.

CHAPTER 8

PEOPLE PLEASING

If you are a people pleaser, you aren't alone. I self-sacrificed and people-pleased for a very long time. It was okay for me to step in and help everyone else, but I felt guilty when I helped myself and when others offered help to me. I laugh about it now, but I used to be so upset about my role in my family.

To give you some background, I was born into an Italian Roman Catholic family, second generation Canadian. My grandparents for the most part only spoke Italian at home. My mom's first language was Italian even though she was born in Canada. Sunday family lunches were my everything. I still remember as a five-year-old when we all lived under one roof (my grandparents, uncle, me, mom, and dad). I would wake up on Sunday to the smell of fresh tomato sauce. Breakfast was a piece of fresh bread dipped in the sauce with a meatball on top, and lunch was homemade pasta. That smell still puts a smile on my face. I fondly remember those times because we would go to church and afterwards, I would sit with my Nonno, my maternal grandfather, and watch "World Wrestling Federation." Together, we watched Hulk Hogan while my Nonna, my maternal grandmother, would be in the kitchen getting lunch ready. She always cooked and cleaned and in her younger years, she worked a full-time job, too. Our Sunday meals were five courses long, and my Nonna was always a course behind in eating. She wouldn't sit with us at the table because she always made sure everyone was well fed. This is the role I thought I was born to play, and that I ended up playing for years: a selfless caregiver, putting the needs of everyone else ahead of me, while sacrificing myself, even if that meant losing myself along the way.

My Italian friends and I joke that we were born with Italian Woman Catholic Guilt First Child Syndrome as soon as we exited the womb. It is our duty to take care of others. To eat last. To clean up after everyone. To hold the pieces together and to put them back together when they fall apart. It's an enormous responsibility, and I hated it. There were times in my late teenage years when I would go to friends' birthday parties and make sure everyone else had enough food before I considered eating. I eventually was labeled the "mom" of my friends' group and later the "Nonna" as well. I took pride in this because I knew what my role was and I stepped into it, doing it well. However, I sacrificed me.

In my twenties, it was no longer just food; I sacrificed my time and energy. I became hyper-independent so I didn't have to ask for help and thought I must be agreeable and go out of my way to get along with everyone. That wasn't the truth, because the truth was I didn't know who I was or who I wanted to be because I thought I needed to fall in line, fit in the crowd, and make everyone else around me happy.

Along with being influenced by my culture, having a father who was angry the majority of the time meant I frequently tried to step in and fix situations to ease the tension. There were times after grade school when I would check to see what my mom didn't have the energy to accomplish during the day so I could speedily do it before my dad got home. Even to this day, the sound of a garage door raises the hair on my arms, and I feel the need to jump up and scan my environment to see what is out of place. My mom's depression was so bad at times she couldn't move from her bed or the couch. When I finally got my driver's license, it became my responsibility to be chauffeur, to take my mom to her doctors' appointments and run errands.

Smoothing conflicts over and compromising my beliefs were the easier ways to accommodate others including family, friends, patients, staff, and guys I dated. I avoided arguments and disagreements to keep the peace, and, in doing so, I tried to guess what others were thinking to stay steps ahead. I didn't realize I was doing this until I had nothing left to give (the full story will be in Part III, Burnout). I became resentful and jealous of others while I became more agreeable and conflict-averse. People could say "no" or "not now" and schedule times in their day to have fun or rest while I was stuck saying "yes" and "right away" and feeling guilty when I took time for myself. My inner narrative had me convinced I wasn't worthy to take care of me and that I didn't matter unless everyone around me was happy.

Halfway through my master's degree, I left because I got into dental school, and my parents finally decided to separate. My dad moved out, and my mom remained at my childhood home. On a weekend in the spring, I was told I had to return home to help with the move because if I stayed at school that would be a sign that I took a side, my mother's side. I didn't want to help move because home didn't feel like a mentally or emotionally safe place for me. Being a people pleaser, I reluctantly went home to be the buffer between two adults and, again, to make everyone else happy, except me.

My mother's final words before I booked the train ticket were, "If you don't go and help, he will blame me and take it out on me."

What I didn't realize at the time was that it wasn't my responsibility to shield my mom, smooth things over with my dad, or act as a buffer. I carried this thought process with me into practicing dentistry, friendships, and dating. I had an unhealthy focus on putting others before myself. It became easy to agree with friends when I didn't want to speak up, or take on more responsibility at work when I no longer had the bandwidth but didn't want to disappoint. Maintaining harmony while dating despite not having my needs met was easier than expressing my feelings and upsetting someone else. Eventually, putting on a smile and sucking it up no longer worked. But this belief of putting others first, minimizing disagreements, and not choosing me started at such an early age that unlearning this took many, many years.

As high-achieving women, we can be taken advantage of when we want to be liked and want things to be perfect. There are times when we do and say things for the sake of agreement and approval because it's easier to be considered helpful and kind. The combination of people-pleasing and perfectionism is destructive, as it calls you to question your self-worth. Just as we discussed fears in relation to perfectionism, fear of rejection or disapproval comes with people-pleasing. **The underlying belief is that if you keep pleasing, achieving, and perfecting, then you will be liked and wanted.**

When I was thirty, I scrolled through one of the dating apps and pondered if I would ever find someone. I had broken up with my ex a couple of years ago, and he was already engaged to the next person. While I was newly single, I explored the dating apps and a couple years later even hired a dating company. It just didn't work out. I always felt alone because I didn't have a partner. I knew I was fine on my own, but I wanted more.

As I write this book at the age of thirty-five, I am still on my own but I see it very differently, and I definitely don't feel alone. Before, I felt like I needed to tone myself down. I subdued my personality and plastered on a smile, especially in clinic and around men, to fit inside a box in the hopes that others would like me, because I have been told on multiple occasions that I'm "too loud." So-called friends, family members, men I've dated, and random people at school, clinic, and conferences have shushed me and used hand gestures, telling me to reduce my volume and intensity. Because of this, I changed how I showed up. It wasn't everyone, and yet those one-off individuals made a dent in my mind, reminding me I'm *too much.* Those individuals reminded me that I should know my place, and to me that meant taking care of others and doing it silently.

In my late twenties, I felt pressured by society and social media and started to feel scared that my eggs were withering away. I felt I had limited time to decide if I wanted to have children. My profession required me to put my personal life on hold, or at least that's what I thought, so I considered freezing an egg or embryo. Without even realizing, I also lowered my expectations of potential partners because I felt like I was a piece of food about to expire. My family never pressured me to have children; however, that pressure as a woman to bear children and use my uterus was still there. When I was a kid, I imagined having my own children but over time that picture faded, and my life vision changed. My entire life was dedicated to helping take care of others and being a parent to my mom, so by the age of thirty I had this burning desire to choose me. However, the guilt of even thinking of myself plagued me.

I remember sitting at the kitchen table having pasta for dinner one day after work. Nonna sat across from me, my mom on my right, and my brother on my left. My mom and I were chatting about freezing an embryo and when a good age to do that would be.

All of a sudden, my Nonna chimed in. "Do you know how much that costs?"

Blinking quizzically, I said, "I do. Do you?"

With an air of being proud, she said, "Yeah, it costs $20,000."

I was shocked. "How do you even know that?"

"I pay attention."

I had no words, but Nonna continued to speak.

"Jessie, you just spent so many years in school. Why not spend money on you? Why not spend money and travel some?"

My jaw was likely on the floor. Here was my Nonna, a strong woman who immigrated to Canada in hopes for a better life and who puts her family and friends first, telling me to take care of *me.*

"Jessie, listen to me, there are a lot of kids in the world who need a home. If you wake up one day when you are older and decide you want a kid, then adopt. Because even if you freeze an egg, you could still end up with one of these two," she said as she pointed to my brother and my mom.

Initially, I was shocked because Nonna dropped some wise words. A large part of why I wanted to freeze an embryo in my late twenties was to prevent the possibility of genetic abnormalities by using a younger egg. However, there is still no guarantee of outcomes. Here I was trying to be perfect and control an outcome not in my control. After the initial shock, not only was my jaw on the floor but I laughed hysterically because Nonna reminded me that both my mom and brother have mental health issues that come with their own challenges. We all laughed together because we understood the struggle. This helped me see a different perspective: I've already been a parent for a while, and I am allowed to not want to have kids as well.

The day my Nonna shocked me and made me laugh was the day I decided to stop worrying about whether or not I was doing things to appease others. It opened my eyes to rethinking how I chose to help. It has taken me years, and at times I still slip back into people-pleasing, but I never froze my eggs because I no longer felt the pressure to please society and global culture. I want to be crystal clear about freezing an egg or an embryo: if you feel it is a good option for you, I support you in making the best possible decision for yourself. Remember, I'm sharing parts of my life, experiences with my clients, and research so you have more information and know that you have options.

Nevertheless, this is what I have learned and want to share with you: it is not your responsibility to make others happy. **It is your**

responsibility to make yourself happy by asking yourself what you truly want. You can bring happiness to others but you can't force them to be happy if they don't choose it. Looking back, it wasn't my actions that would have helped any of those situations or people; it was others who needed to figure out their own shit. They put it on me and then I made it mine to fix when it was never mine to fix to begin with.

Harper, an owner of a medium-sized organization and a client of mine, was getting ready to sell her portion of the business. She felt it was time to explore other interests and step into a different opportunity. She had wanted this for ages but didn't want to disappoint her business partner or clients by shifting out of her current position. She stayed a lot longer than she wanted because she was more concerned about what others would think of her than what she wanted for herself.

Many women stay stuck in jobs for fear of the uncomfortable conversations—deciding to resign, asking for a raise, or offering suggestions for improvements. **Being a people pleaser protects against what others will say and do, however, it also means you stay in the same position: not stepping into your voice or full potential.**

Over the last couple of years, I have helped a number of women leave their jobs. When these women started working with me, their goal wasn't to resign but to be happier and less stressed. Through coaching, these women could finally see themselves for who they are: strong, powerful, competent, smart, capable, and more than enough. When they started to change their inner voice which changed the way they viewed themselves, they were able to accurately assess their environments that had toxic leadership and management. This is why IP, perfectionism, and people pleasing can keep you stuck. When you don't believe in your capabilities, it is easy to think you alone are the problem, because as the high achiever, it's easier to blame yourself than it is to question what is going on around you.

I was with Harper during the initial stages of the big shift from full-time to part-time owner. During this transition she reduced her days and hired someone to take more of her day-to-day responsibilities: overseeing employees, running meetings, and managing operating systems. It was time for Harper to step into her new business, a not-for-profit organization she started from scratch.

On one of our calls, Harper pleaded, "You need to help me with saying 'no.' Since we last spoke, I've said 'yes' to two more speaking engagements."

Harper was notorious for saying yes because she felt bad saying no and didn't want to disappoint others.

I asked, "Are these speaking engagements you wanted to do?"

A heavy sigh. "No."

"Then why did you say yes?"

"What will they think of me? Will they think that I'm too good for them? What if they don't ask me back again because I said no?"

Outside of potentially disappointing others, the high-achieving woman can obsess over each opportunity as the thing that makes a complete difference in her life. She forgets to take into account what *she* wants to be doing.

I'm all for signing up to write a chapter of a book, be an interviewee, or organize a wellness event, but if you keep saying yes, then over time that feeling of overwhelm becomes the prominent emotion. It turns into having to just get through something to reach the next achievement instead of enjoying what you said "yes" to.

Together Harper and I role played what saying "no" would be like. We went over example emails, texts, and in-person conversations. We even practiced the silence that may come *after* her response. That can be a challenge to sit through because it always feels longer than it actually is; justifying why we are saying "no" is definitely easier. Avoid assuming the other person thinks poorly of you; they are likely reflecting on their own thoughts. But answering "no" is a complete sentence.

Harper struggled with saying no entirely, so initially we started with "no, not now," and "let me think on this and get back to you by next week." This gave Harper the opportunity to step away and really ask herself if this opportunity was right for her.

TIPS TO AVOID PEOPLE PLEASING

1. Identify your wants. Ask yourself what you really want. Not just what you *need* but what you *want*!
2. Define your priorities. These could be people, yourself, or goals. When you define who, what, and where your priorities are, it becomes easier to follow tip #5.
3. Be diligent with boundaries (we will go over boundaries in Part III, Burnout).
4. Give yourself time to explore all possibilities. Set a date and time by which you will get back to them. Avoid feeling rushed to make a decision. Check your calendar, remind yourself of your wants, and then make the decision. Remember, when you aren't making a decision, you use energy subconsciously; sitting and stewing keeps you from enjoying your everyday life.
5. Say "no" with conviction and don't justify. Avoid over-explaining or giving excuses in hopes to ease your discomfort of saying no. When you say "no," be proud. When you are saying "no" to someone, you are saying "yes" to someone else: yourself.
6. Don't apologize, especially if it's not your fault. You can definitely say "thank you," but do not apologize. There is nothing to be sorry about. You do not have to be sorry for choosing you.

7. Know that you can't be perfect and make everyone happy. You will not be perfect to everyone because perfection is a perspective. Be what you need to be for yourself and the people of priority. Own your imperfections.

PART III
BURNOUT

“They asked her,
‘How do you love yourself well?’
She answered:
‘Make your well-being and
healing a top priority. Have the
courage to create boundaries that
will support your flourishing. Listen
closely to your intuition, respect
your need for rest and connect with
people who are emotionally mature.
Being intentional with your life is loving
yourself well.’”
—*Yung Pueblo, poet, author, speaker*

CHAPTER 9

WHAT IS BURNOUT?

I don't know about you but the first two parts of this book were eye-opening for me. They made me realize that for years and years, even decades, I made a choice to accept the negative ways I spoke to myself. There was no way I would speak to another human being like that, yet all those hateful words came out and criticized me! It felt natural because I had convinced myself everyone spoke to themselves like that, so it was okay for me to do it, too. Little did I know the impact it was having on my mental, physical, emotional, and spiritual self.

As I've discussed in earlier chapters, a large part of my life has been mitigating family drama, being a caregiver, and trying to fix everything and everyone around me. I believed if I kept the peace, then making others happy would be my job. It's the role I took on from when I was a child and accepted wholeheartedly until the moment I broke inside.

A norm for me since I was a kid was attending my mom's psychiatry appointments both at the request of her and her doctor. I dreaded these appointments, just another thing to do for someone else while I would rather be elsewhere. As soon as I got my license, I was the one to drive her there. Thankfully, attending one of her appointments saved my life.

As usual, I arrived early, because I could never be late to appointments, events, or gatherings. As a kid, arriving late meant my father would erupt into anger, or I would walk on eggshells because he was pissed. Eventually, when I became a practicing dentist, running on time was my nemesis. I didn't want to disappoint my assistant, my receptionist, or the patient. However, that pressure to make everyone else around me happy—my father, my patients and staff, friends and family—meant I spent hours of my life arriving early and twiddling my thumbs. My inner critic convinced me that if I arrived late, then the other person would be mad at me, someone would hate me, or I would have ruined everything. I was in this massive spiral of deprecation, disapproval, and self-destruction.

Burnout is the "disconnection between what people are and what they have to do. It represents the crumbling of your value, dignity, and spirit."[28] It doesn't happen overnight, which means it also won't go away overnight. It is gradual and continuous; sometimes you don't even know it is happening to you if you go through the motions without reflecting or listening to your mind and body. Dr. Maslach, who coined the term in 1982, describes it as "an erosion of the human soul."

Damn, those are powerful words: "an erosion of the human soul." It now makes sense why I felt like I was in a deep, dark abyss. In 2019, the World Health Organization defined burnout as an occupational phenomenon, resulting from chronic workplace stress that is not managed.[29]

That day at the psychiatrist office, when I had taken my mom to her appointment, I was diagnosed with burnout, clinical depression, and a generalized anxiety disorder, at the age of twenty-nine. Prior to these diagnoses, I didn't realize what I was experiencing. *Burnout* wasn't a buzzword like it is now in our culture and society. I had an inkling something was wrong, but I didn't comprehend to what extent. My mother is bipolar, so I knew what depression looked like and I wasn't experiencing that. Me, the high achiever, high performer, high-functioning woman could manage through a little sadness here and there. I believed whatever was being thrown my way made me stronger and that I would be fine, so: challenge accepted.

I can already tell you the challenge failed and here's why—that inner critic in my head kept me from acknowledging something was wrong by saying things like "You don't need help; there are others worse off" and "You are getting up and going to work so you are fine." And my favourite: "Suck it up, Buttercup." The reality was that I only functioned in survival mode. From the moment I woke up, I already wished to be back in bed. Moving through the day seemed normal but I was only going through the motions with no end in sight. It felt like Groundhog Day every day: get up, wish the day away, go to work, come home, bombard my thoughts and senses with TV, overeat, and drink wine or tequila so I didn't have to feel anything. My thoughts and inner critic were so pessimistic and cynical that feeling numb was better than the alternative.

During graduate school, I lived by semesters, where at the end of every four months there was a mental break and fresh start. Each semester meant I got to try again. When I finally graduated dental school, it meant there were no more semesters. I was supposed to work for the next thirty straight years. I started to explore hobbies and find new interests because that's what I was told to do; however, I did them with my eyes glazed over. For years, even my social life felt disconnected, and dinners with friends felt empty and void. My stomach was always in knots and had butterflies, not the good kind, which made me feel constantly nauseated. I lost a lot of weight because the anxiety churned and tightened my stomach. Each meal was torture because I knew I needed to eat but I couldn't stomach my food; so, I chose not to eat.

I started to wish away the next thirty years of my career, only so I could get to retirement. Because then that's when I would be happy . . . right? Society, culture, family, and the adults around me promoted retirement as if it was this magical award you had to get to feel happiness, contentment, and joy. If you have ever played *The Game of Life,* it is literally set up exactly for this. To win, you need to get to retirement. But as a general dentist who treats cancer patients, I have since learned not everyone makes it.

Throughout my initial years of practicing as a dentist, I fed myself lies, saying that one day in the future, I would wake up feeling healthy, happy, and successful. So, I kept burning the candle at both ends, working around the clock, filling every hour with something to do even if that meant sacrificing my sleep and rest. I had convinced myself that by doing all the right things, eventually my life would be better and I would feel happy. Well, that was utterly wrong because my inner critic would push me and never let me enjoy retirement even if I made it there. If I kept going at the rate I was going, I would have dug my own grave.

Back in Part I, I talked about moving your goal post over the cognitive horizon. Let me explain why that makes you feel less and less satisfied. Picture a mountain you are ready to climb, with your goal at the top. You decide what that goal is, and you pack your backpack and get ready to scale that mountain. The journey up the mountain can be long and time-consuming, but reaching your first goal feels incredible. You look out at the view and revel in how far you've come. This first goal was easy to embody and recognize, but you, as a high achiever, also like the challenge of setting goals. On your way back down, that first goal is no longer enough to make you happy, so you decide you want to set another goal. And you do. You plan, pack your backpack, and start to scale again. You make it to the top, but this time, it doesn't feel as exciting or thrilling as last time. You look out across the mountains and see the next mountain, the next goal, and you want to climb there before you even start heading down.

After the second mountain, you get ready for your third. Now you're a wee bit antsy. You already want to be at the top.

You frantically pack your bag and head out, and this time you trip over some rocks, snag your jacket on a tree branch, get lost, and spot a bear. Ascending the third mountain doesn't feel worth it anymore, as it becomes challenging with new experiences, but that view at the top keeps you going. Before reaching the summit, you think, "This mountain wasn't the greatest, so the next one will be better." You've already moved onto the fourth and fifth mountains, imagining a better, more fulfilling journey and view. The thrill and excitement wear off. Ascending becomes a means to an end. The only excitement passing through you is the thought the next mountain will be the one that makes everything better. Your goal post continues to move over the cognitive horizon, which you never reach. Eventually you get stuck in a loop of never-ending numbness, despair, and resentment, especially when you see other people's journeys and mountains on social media, which convinces you that your mountains are never enough.

So what should you do instead? You have to enjoy the walk down just as much as you enjoyed scaling up. It's in the walk down that you savour your success. If you run down your mountain and rush through the success, this can keep you stuck in the impostor cycle when you start to climb your next mountain. **Make time to enjoy this new achieved goal, success, or happiness before you automatically jump to the next.** Constantly moving the cognitive horizon can leave you overextended, stressed, exhausted, cynical, and doubtful which over time can lead you to Burnout Mountain.

Achieving was never going to make me happy. Reaching that next goal wasn't going to fill the growing void in my head, heart, and soul. Every day my inner critic spoke to me was another day it pushed my inner cheerleader deep into that darkness where she was too scared to speak or be seen. My inner critic was a full-blown trickster, telling me that I liked everything perfect, that I had to work hard, that being productive meant I was succeeding, and that taking care of others would bring me the utmost joy.

Research has shown that experiencing IP is linked to experiencing perfectionism. Perfectionism breeds self-judgement, which affects how you perceive your worth (based on what your inner critic is saying). **Experiencing IP and perfectionism together is one of the strongest predictors of psychological distress, which can lead to burnout.**[30 31 32 33]

What you believe you deserve is based on what your inner critic has convinced you of. "You deserve that shitty job because you won't qualify for a promotion." "You deserve to sit in the audience instead of being on stage." "You deserve to stay in that shitty relationship because no one else will think you are enough." And the list goes on. **Burnout for the high achiever is preventable if and only if they create an awareness of how they choose to speak to themselves and recognize the pressures and expectations they believe they need to live up to.** Long story short: you are doing this to yourself.

Let me be very clear as I start to describe burnout: if you have changed the way you speak to yourself and implemented self-care practices for a period of time but are still not feeling better, then the problem is no longer you, it's your environment. Your environment is a crucial part of navigating burnout. For example, if you keep quitting your job, hoping the next job will be more fulfilling but you haven't done the internal work, then it may not be the environment. Instead, it may be your inner critic and your unhealthy patterns. When you do the internal work, you can accurately assess why the environment isn't working and go about looking for what needs to be changed within your environment.

What exactly is burnout? Burnout is broken down into three components:

1. FEELINGS OF ENERGY DEPLETION OR EXHAUSTION

This is the feeling of fatigue by stress of work or your personal life, and it is the progressive loss of energy mentally and emotionally. This can present as physical symptoms as well, including but not limited to stomach ulcers, chronic fatigue, headaches, acid reflux, insomnia, sleep disturbances, and more.

2. FEELINGS OF NEGATIVITY OR CYNICISM RELATED TO YOUR JOB

This is the development of negative attitudes and irritability toward the people around you, including work colleagues, family, and friends. Under this category is compassion fatigue, which is experiencing decreased empathy due to chronic emotional strain. It can leave you feeling powerless and full of dread. Now remember, we've already talked about how perfectionists like control over their outcomes and environments. With uncertainty, our mind wants answers, which we are unable to find while experiencing negativity and cynicism. Caring is hard, and without proper boundaries, caring too much means you lose yourself in the process.

3. FEELING A LACK OF PERSONAL ACCOMPLISHMENT

This is where your confidence takes a hit. I believe this is why your inner critic's voice becomes more noticeably glaring as that trickster. It is in these moments when you no longer think you are good enough and you don't have the energy to fight your inner critic's negativity. Instead, you accept it at face value and no longer have the strength to find evidence of your past accomplishments. When you lose your confidence, day-to-day activities become hard, and you may experience decreased productivity. I'm not talking about production value in terms of money, I'm talking about the fact that it's hard to get going and stay going. It's hard to get out of bed, it's hard to take a shower, it's hard to move, it's hard to make decisions.

To me, burnout feels like you're constantly living in survival mode without an off-switch and without the resources to adequately feel successful. Over time, you experience nervous system dysregulation, because humans are not meant to live in survival mode for an extended period of time. As a reminder, survival mode is our fight-or-flight and freeze response (FF response). Let's take the time now to break down burnout, anxiety, stress, and worry. The media throws around and interchanges these terms, so many people don't understand the difference. I'll go through each of these items in depth, but first, here is the equation of how they interrelate:

Anxiety = Stress + Worry

Anxiety is the combination of stress and worry, whereas *stress* is the physical component which I like to call our "bodyset." It is a primitive region of our brain, the amygdala, so ancient that it gets immediately activated, like a knee-jerk reflex, when we are figuring out if we are, in fact, safe. It is a protective mechanism hardwired in our brains so we can live and survive. It is innate, always scanning for danger around us. If it finds what it perceives as danger, then it activates our sympathetic nervous system, which is our FF response. For example, back in the day, we feared lions and tigers and bears (oh my!); actually, I live in British Columbia now so I still fear bears out on my hikes, but I digress. When activated, the amygdala starts a chain of events, turning on other parts of our brain to keep us safe. It also examines our surroundings and pushes the information to our thinking brain, the prefrontal cortex, to keep us alive. If you were out foraging and you came across a potential plant that looked delicious, but your friend ate it and they died, then you would commit that plant to memory. Then, any time you saw that plant you might get tense, as the amygdala reminds you not to eat it. Stress is a normal biological response to perceived threat.

Worry is the psychological response, which I will call your "mindset." Worrying is just as important as our stress response, because it helps our mind start a chain of events like problem-solving and critical thinking. We worry in order to find answers to the questions we have, and this helps calm the brain. Worrying is a normal biological response if it leads to change and helps you find answers. It can become detrimental if you find yourself overthinking or having obsessive thoughts. **If you call yourself a worrier or a catastrophizer, or if you experience IP, your baseline to calm down has been altered.** It takes more time and energy to calm your mind; your brain requires more proof and potentially also your perfectionist behaviours to ease the worry. If we add onto the poisonous plant example from above, being a catastrophizer would mean you think all new plants could cause harm, and it becomes difficult to distinguish between information gathering and anxiousness from past experience.

THE BREAKDOWN OF STRESS AND WORRY

Anxiety = Stress + Worry	
Stress:	Worry:
Physical (Bodyset)	Psychological (Mindset)
Heart racing, trembling, sweating, chest tightness, dry mouth, butterflies in stomach or upset stomach, rapid breathing or shallow breathing	Thinking thoughts, problem solving, critical thinking
Both are normal biological responses	

So, if anxiety is the combination of stress and worry, then anxiety is like a smoke detector. Smoke can be from a fire, or smoke could be because of the crumbles at the bottom of a toaster. This makes you think your toast is burning when it isn't actually burning. You can experience anxiety at two different times where both your bodyset and your mindset are activated: before and during the anxious event.

Research has shown that your level of anxiety *before* an event is greater than the level of anxiety *during* an event.[34] [35] The lead-up to doing your taxes, especially if you put it off, causes more distress and anxiety than when you actually sit down and do your taxes. Your mind and thoughts can activate an intense stress response in your bodyset. When you continue to experience chronic anxiety, your "gut reaction" or intuition is now tangled. It is no longer truly reliable. When you're getting ready to do your taxes, you start to feel like something is going to go wrong, and because you trust your intuition, you put off your taxes for fear you are unsafe.

In moments like this, your inner critic turns on and says, "Yup, you're right, your bodyset is reacting because you aren't good enough to do your taxes. Let's put them off until we absolutely have to." The inner critic's voice is that trickster that uses our amygdala, the primitive ancient part of our mind, against us. When the inner critic links negative self-talk to the FF response, then we start to believe that feeling uncomfortable when doing our taxes is bad, and that we should avoid it at all costs.

That discomfort is *only* your FF response. This is fascinating because this is what prevents us from growing and learning. Your inner voice uses a perceived threat, whether real or feared, to convince yourself that you aren't capable. Your inner critic's words now get linked to your FF response, convincing you that you can't do your taxes. I realize I have stuck with the example of taxes, but you can replace it with a meeting, performance, presentation, procedure, dating, dinners, people pleasing, perfectionism, and so on. To get unstuck, it is important to differentiate between true physical threats and what your inner critic thinks you can't do.

Stress itself does not cause burnout. Stress can intensify burnout over time but it may not be the main cause of burnout. Burnout does not happen overnight, nor is it an acute response. It is gradual and continuous over a period of time where you are exposed to extended periods of anxiety that go unmanaged with a lack of resources in your environment.

Let's review: *anxiety* is the combination of *stress,* which is the reaction in your bodyset, and *worry,* which is the reaction in your mindset. Stressors or stressful events can activate your anxiety *before* and *during* the event, where *before* can elicit a more intense set of emotions and thoughts. A stressor can be a person, place, or thing. Burnout is not stress. Burnout is chronic and complex.

BRAIN TRAINING EXERCISE: UNDERSTANDING STRESSORS

1. List a potential stressor (person, place, thing, or experience). How does it make you feel in your bodyset and mindset?
2. What if you thought of it as a problem? How would that affect your bodyset and mindset?
3. What if you thought of it as a challenge? How would that affect your bodyset and mindset?
4. What if you thought of it as an opportunity? How would that affect your bodyset and mindset?

When you pay attention to how a stressor affects your mind and body, you can start to pay attention to that connection you have created. If you can shift the way you think about the stressor, you can affect how your bodyset and mindset respond. This is extremely powerful because the shift is based on your word choice. If you see your stressor as a problem, you may feel your heart beat faster and you start to sweat. But if you see your stressor as an opportunity, this connects with your mind and body differently. And all we changed was a word.

A number of my clients come to me saying their "anxiety came out of nowhere" and now they feel like they can't control it anymore. The idea that anxiety comes out of nowhere is a massive misconception. Let me also remind you that anxiety and burnout are not the same thing. I usually ask my clients to describe the anxiety attack they experienced or when they experienced peak anxiety. My clients usually tell me: "I was doing something regular and all of a sudden it consumed me. I couldn't think clearly and I felt like I couldn't control my thoughts or what was happening to me." I get that. It feels like it came out of nowhere, but trust me, it doesn't.

Picture this: we each have an anxiety container.[36] Think of it like a jar or container with a lid. Throughout our entire lives, our conscious and subconscious mind constantly decides and categorizes what is and what isn't a stressor that causes anxiety. Over time, the container starts to fill with stressors: relationships, finances, work and home obligations, deciding whether or not to have children, pressure around school events or kids' hobbies, and so on. Your inner critic can amplify these stressors, making you perceive them as worse and worse.

When you were younger, there was more than enough room in the anxiety container to hold all your stressors. When your mind defined a stressor, the lid opened and in it went. As you continued to put more and more pressure on yourself, you started to jam the stressors into the jar, eventually leaving no room for unpacking earlier stressors or giving yourself the time and clarity to understand why they were stressors to begin with. Like, why does my anxiety container still hold onto that time in elementary school when I stood under the basketball net and the ball landed on my head and I was super embarrassed? If we don't understand the stressor and why it stays in the container, then we don't create space for new stressors to come into our life.

Eventually, the container no longer has more room and the lid will pop off. So, what actually causes it? Well, it's the dinner that accidentally gets burnt, or tripping over your shoes, or a comment from that one colleague. It was building up all along, reached a tipping point, and then your inner critic reminded you that "you're a loser for not being able to manage it all." Thanks for nothing, inner critic.

When you start to manage what your inner critic says, then you can sit with your thoughts in the quiet and unpack those stressors one by one. There is no longer a fear to be alone with your inner voice or thoughts. Examining each stressor and understanding why it's still in your jar allows you to create additional space for unplanned stressors, like your car breaking down, getting injured while working out, or someone standing you up on a date. When your anxiety container has room for the unexpected, then it doesn't feel like it's the worst day, month, or year.

Let me take you back to my mother's appointment. As I sat in the psychiatrist's waiting room, my mother strolled in with two large shopping bags. At this point, my mom was manic. I knew this already by how our phone conversations and texts were going. I could also see it in her eyes and demeanor when I would visit for Sunday lunch. At the appointment was when I would describe, in detail, how manic she was so her psychiatrist could adjust her medications accordingly. A portion of my mom's mania includes spending money on things she really doesn't need. Today's shopping spree: socks, underwear, and pants. Now, I know what you're thinking: "Jessica, that doesn't sound so bad." You're right, it's not so bad if it stopped there. But that's not how mania works. This time, thankfully, it was only socks, underwear, and pants. Previous purchases had been more grandiose.

As I sat in the psychiatrist's waiting room, watching my mom walk in with multiple shopping bags, I could feel tears welling up in my eyes. Instinctually I whispered to myself, *Suck it up. You're the caregiver. Don't be weak.* And I did. I blinked away my tears, held my breath while I decided to put a cork in it, and quickly said, "Let's see what the doctor has to say."

We waited in silence until we were called into the room and took our seats. I sat as far away from my mom as I could, the shopping bags between us. My mom started talking and I could tell it was like her brain was moving faster than the speed of light. I looked over at her doctor, and he caught my eye and knew something was up. He turned to me and asked, "What's been going on?"

I couldn't shove the emotions down anymore. Tears started pricking my eyes, the knot in my chest got tighter, and I thought I was going to vomit. Finding words was difficult. He looked at my mom, who was expressionless, a normal state during her mania. When you had conversations with her it was as if she looked right through you into her own world.

The psychiatrist then looked back at me and briefly asked how work was going. I responded, "It's challenging to treat cancer patients, but I enjoy it" as I wiped my tears.

He asked, "What are you doing outside of work?"

I crumbled, "I don't have energy to do anything."

In that moment he leaned forward and said, "Jessica, I think it's time for you to come and see me on your own. I think you are experiencing burnout, depression, and anxiety."

Through the nausea, tears, and chest tightness, I mumbled, "Okay." I didn't have the strength to say that "I was fine and today was a bad day" because, let's be real, it wasn't just today. I couldn't keep living like this, nor did I want to keep living like this. I knew something needed to change. I was used to holding everything and everyone together, until I couldn't. The moment my psychiatrist recommended an antidepressant and anti-anxiety medication, I felt a wave of shame flood me. I thought this couldn't and shouldn't be me because I was the doctor helping others. This was a huge turning point for me. As I tried to outrun my own mental health concerns, I ran right into a brick wall.

A large part of why I didn't reach out prior to this was because of my inner voice. I thought I had to have it all together. I was now a dentist. On the outside I was joyful and cheerful, and I laughed ALL the time. Yet, on the inside I was full of sadness, anxiousness, frustration, shame, regret, and envy.

Jessica, you're fine is what the inner critic convinced me, over and over again. I eventually believed it. I worked a full-time job, volunteered on multiple dental committees locally, provincially, and nationally, was trying to find Mr. Right, and started jiu jitsu and sailing. I was fine because I checked all the boxes. I was doing everything right, wasn't I? My inner critic kept pushing me harder and harder, telling me to do more and be more because what I was doing was not enough.

Here's the thing: I thought I knew what depression looked like, and crying about my life while sitting in front of the TV, hung over, was not that. Or so I thought. To me, depression was not being able to get out of bed or get dressed in the morning. It was sitting in front of the TV all day and mindlessly zoning out all day every day. I was doing all the right things so I didn't fit into what I thought depression, anxiety, or burnout looked like. Just because you have one doesn't mean you have all three; each diagnosis has its unique characteristics. They can be interrelated at times, like how it was for me. However, understanding what affects you personally is important so you can determine what you specifically need for healing.

At the time, not knowing there were different types of burnout kept me from asking for help. Sure, I definitely experienced workplace burnout, but then there was caregiver burnout—chronic stress that came from taking care of a loved one, the endless exhaustion, feeling overwhelmed by my caregiver responsibilities, and believing no matter what I did I failed at all my roles. Reflecting back, that was me. I was completely depleted of energy and was chronically exhausted. Burnout is commonly thought of as job-related, but there is also parental burnout, relationship burnout, underchallenged burnout and what I experienced, caregiver burnout. These types of burnout are not well known, nor widely talked about, making it difficult for any woman to recognize what is going on. As a result, women will blame themselves more often for fear of stereotype and stigma.

Around the same time I was diagnosed with burnout, I developed painful acid reflux that kept me up at night and forced me to sleep sitting up. Lying down made my heart feel on fire, eventually requiring a stomach lining biopsy. I became so cynical toward my mother, my patients, and the people around me who had good boundaries. I asked myself, *Why are they allowed to take breaks? Create a schedule they enjoy? Do work that they love?*

And talking about that lack of personal accomplishment, I had zero confidence—zilch, nada, absolutely nothing. There were days I didn't want to take a shower because water droplets felt like tiny spikes hitting my skin. Lastly, if I wasn't keeping myself busy with work, jiu jitsu or hanging out with friends, then I was in fact, a blob. Because I was constantly busy, I justified why I was unable to move from the couch. In reality, though, I no longer watched TV; the TV watched me as I sat in a void where the only thing I could hear was my inner critic shaming me for being disgusting.

This is what burnout and depression looked like for me, and yet from the outside, I thought I was doing everything right so I *shouldn't* be feeling the way I felt. The pressure I put on myself as that high achiever was my own doing. But I want to share some amazing news: **burnout is recognizable, treatable, and reversible.** However, and this is a big fat however, it can take anywhere from one to four years to get out of burnout.[37] [38] I've looked through enough research, and the range is wide for a couple of reasons. First, not a lot of research exists for long-term studies, especially for the years since the World Health Organization titled burnout a workplace phenomenon in 2019. Second, **a large component of recovery depends on the individuals themselves and the changes they choose to make over a specific length of time.**

If you find yourself regressing or finding comfort in old habits, then it will take longer to grow and learn. This isn't wrong, nor should you belittle yourself. Each opportunity can be used for changing something that isn't working for you. Regardless, do not be afraid of the recovery length. The takeaway is: moving through burnout is not easy, there is no magic pill or quick fix, but it is 100 percent possible. The moment you decide you've had enough and are ready to make those changes is the first day of a journey you will not regret.

Now that I've distinguished the difference between burnout, stress, anxiety, and worry, I really want to explain the difference between experiencing acute stressful events and chronic burnout. **When you experience an acute stressful event, the FF response activates physical symptoms and produces urgency and hyperactivity.** It turns on your reactive emotions like worrying so you can problem solve and critically think. This creates a temporary adaptation in your mindset and bodyset. That temporary adaptation adjusts according to the changing situations, allowing you to step into that event and figure out what you need to figure out. Your mindset and bodyset performed successfully and adequately. ***Chronic burnout, by contrast,* is the combination of physical and emotional symptoms that produce a feeling of helplessness—it is a blunted state.** Instead of experiencing a temporary adaptation, you get a breakdown in your FF response, causing you to deviate from your normal mindset and bodyset functioning. It's a failure to cope. Okay, you are not the failure. I want to make sure you separate you being the failure from your nervous system shutting down. When your nervous system isn't able to function properly or is dysregulated, that's when we feel like we are always putting out fires or waiting for the shoe to drop while we sit in survival mode. In order to cope and manage hopelessness or helplessness, the next step is avoidance and wanting to escape the discomfort. This can come in the form of numbing behaviours, which will be discussed in the next chapter.

MINDSET AND BODYSET: CHRONIC BURNOUT SYMPTOMS

Burnout	
Mindset	Bodyset
Depressed or changing moods, tearfulness, helplessness (loss of hope), feelings of powerlessness or of being trapped, sense of failure, poor self-esteem, guilt, inability to concentrate, and boredom	Headaches, nausea, dizziness, muscle and joint pain, sleep disturbances, insomnia, gastrointestinal ulcers and disorders, chronic fatigue and more

If you connected with the mindset and bodyset of burnout, then I want to say you are not alone. A lot of high achievers move through life not realizing they are in burnout. Instead, these women believe if they just keep going then something will change and eventually they will feel better, or that this is normal and they should be feeling all of these things. The latter is not true; you do not need to stay in burnout to thrive.

If you think back to the anxiety container, there are two different visuals you can think of: the lid popping off and constant overflow. The lid popping off is a sudden snap or acute reaction, known as an anxiety attack. When the lid is off and anxiety constantly overflows, I like to think of it as burnout. There is no end in sight, and as hard as you try to keep all the items in the container, they just keep pouring out.

When you change your inner dialogue from critic to cheerleader, understand and reflect on your stressors, and make yourself a priority, not only do you unpack what is in the anxiety container, but your container starts to take on a new shape. Your capacity to manage stressors has transformed.

BRAIN TRAINING EXERCISE: DRAW YOUR ANXIETY CONTAINER

I know I just gave you a lot of information to digest—a lot of awesome information, but a lot, nonetheless. So, let's do a fun little exercise I like to do with my clients. Grab a blank piece of paper. Draw a decently sized square and start to write in your stressors. They could be finances, travel, work, relationships, etc. Get really specific. For example, a stressor might be booking your dental cleaning appointment. Maybe that's been nagging at you, and committing time to it has added stress because you don't know where it will fit in. Or, maybe you said "yes" to a family member that you didn't want to say "yes" to and it's adding more stress. Whatever comes to mind, write it down and put it into the box. You can do this all in one sitting or you can do this over a couple of days. That way the stressors that didn't immediately present themselves come to your mind eventually.

Easy-peasy, right? Now why did I have you do this exercise?

If there are more stressors than you can fit inside the square, then this is a good indication it's time to unpack those stressors to truly understand why they give you anxiety instead of just jamming them in there and hoping for the best. If you are stressing out about what size the square should be, don't. I didn't give dimensions because I want you to draw whatever came to mind.

You can redefine your stressors by changing your inner voice, resetting expectations, creating healthy habits, and establishing boundaries. As we round out Part III, we will be going over numbing behaviors in the next chapter, and then I'll teach you how to create healthy habits and establish boundaries.

CHAPTER 10

NUMBING BEHAVIOURS

It was a Sunday afternoon and I had already been sitting in front of the TV for six hours. I drank too much the night before and vomited a couple of times throughout the night. I also had fallen asleep with a blanket on the bathroom floor because the tiles felt cool against my skin. The sensation eased my nausea. At two o'clock in the afternoon, I still sipped on an electrolyte drink, felt like crap, and looked like crap.

Weekends became a space in time where I would "let loose" because of how hard I worked during the week. It was a justification to drink as much as I did. Drinking numbed my pain for a period of time, and I became the fun-loving woman I so desperately wanted to be. That fun-loving woman was no different than my usual self. The only difference was the alcohol made me believe it. My inner cheerleader full of liquid courage would tell me I was beautiful, successful, capable, and surrounded by incredible people. But the next day during my hangover, my inner critic was always louder than drunk inner cheerleader, as it reminded me I would never be good enough.

The day after I drank was something I looked forward to because it meant I was finally able to rest. I had to do a lot of processing over the years to understand why I overconsumed, and a large part of that was because when I felt like absolute garbage, I'd finally allow myself to rest. Being a hard worker, striving for perfection, wanting others to like me, and fulfilling my family obligations meant I wasn't allowed to take a break. Rest and breaks were for the weak. I had to keep moving because then my inner critic wouldn't be as loud.

Numbing behaviours are actions or habits that help you escape reality, or zone out, so you don't have to feel bad, sad, or uncomfortable. It's a way to suppress your FF response and worrying. If perfectionist behaviours protect you from failure by causing you to push yourself, then numbing behaviours protect you by numbing you.

Numbing behaviours can include excessive shopping, scrolling social media, alcohol and substance abuse, binge-watching TV, online games, and revenge bedtime procrastination, to name a few. You may even catch yourself doing more than one thing at the same time. This is done to confuse our senses so you never truly have to feel uncomfortable or be alone with your thoughts or voice. I know from experience that it is easy to sit in front of a crappy show you didn't really want to watch to begin with, grab your phone, and scroll through social media to fill the void of not liking the show but not wanting to think or feel.

It was easy for me on the weekend to convince myself I deserved a glass of wine and shots of tequila because the week was so tough. Having that glass of wine or tequila would mean I accomplished my goal that week of working myself into the ground. My inner critic egged me on, too. *Have that extra glass, then you'll feel better.* But I never did. I never felt better. Instead, my inner critic taunted my inner cheerleader, only keeping her at bay for longer and longer periods of time.

I want to be very clear when it comes to some of these numbing behaviours. Binge-watching a TV show you have looked forward to is completely fine in my books. That is a choice you consciously make. If you look forward to enjoying your favourite show with a bag of popcorn while cuddling with your puppy on a Saturday afternoon for four hours, then, damn it, woman, go ahead and do it. But that type of binging is different from the one where you open your streaming service, spend twenty minutes scrolling to potentially find something you like, eventually settle on something you aren't really happy with, and end up watching multiple episodes because you can't bring yourself to function in any other way.

Revenge bedtime procrastination is when you put off bedtime even when you're tired and you know you should go to bed. This happens when you feel like you didn't have much control over your day or you overworked. If you feel like you don't have control, then you need to get it from somewhere. That somewhere is usually right before bed. You convince yourself to have one more glass of wine, or scroll social media for a bit longer, or watch that one extra episode of TV, or play video games for one more hour. However, putting off bedtime doesn't change the time you wake up in the morning. You still have to get up and go to work, or if you're like me on the weekends, you still get up at the exact same time as you do during the week. In essence, you stole from your sleep and your rest. In the long-term, you're only hurting yourself.

Another client of mine didn't discover she used numbing behaviours until she got pregnant. When Briella and I first started working together before her pregnancy, her biggest concern was she felt like she needed to go back to school to get another certificate. Another certificate meant she would be more confident, right? Wrong. Another certificate, another degree, another set of letters after your name isn't going to make you feel more confident if your inner critic is still allowed to terrorize you. This is impostor phenomenon at its finest.

Fun fact from the tech company Hewlett-Packard: when they were interested in why top management positions didn't have more women in the roles, they discovered women apply for jobs when they meet 100 percent of the qualifications while men apply when they meet only 60 percent. I bring this up because when you get another certificate and you still don't feel more confident, your numbing behaviours provide a false sense of relief.

Briella was a first-time mom and found her first trimester difficult. She was constantly nauseated and uncomfortable, developed acid reflux, and had challenges sleeping.

Any time our physical body doesn't feel well, it is easy for the inner critic to make itself known and exert itself. It can use those moments of discomfort that prey on your insecurities and vulnerabilities. That's why your inner critic continues to be a trickster. You've heard this voice for so long and it's quite familiar, but it hasn't really been helping you along the way.

During Briella's first trimester she stopped drinking coffee and alcohol, for obvious reasons, and during her second trimester she ran less often due to pelvic floor dysfunction. Briella was joyful about her pregnancy yet frustrated. All of the things that brought her joy on a regular basis—coffee, alcohol, running—she couldn't use. It was during this time that Briella recognized every night after a bad day of work, she would convince herself she deserved a glass of wine. Now she had to figure out another way to de-stress and actively sit with her inner critic, instead of drowning its voice with a glass of wine. Processing and embracing the uncomfortable emotions when shitstorms happen allows you to unpack the anxiety container and teach your FF response that it isn't necessary to react. That glass of wine may soothe for a short period of time, but long term it just means the lid will eventually pop off the anxiety container.

Briella hated she couldn't run since that was one space she used to clear her mind. Sometimes she pushed herself too hard because her inner critic would convince her that she wasn't capable elsewhere or failed at something during the day. The days she pushed her running limits were days she came home, crashed on the couch, or potentially injured herself.

As that high achiever, it is easy to push your limits to the max because you know you are capable. But it is just as important to understand when, where, and how you push those limits so you don't break yourself in the process. **You can't improve yourself if you are constantly reasoning with your inner critic that you only deserve something if you beat yourself up first.** Your inner critic has been given the opportunity to be unkind to yourself for some time now. As we continue to rewrite the narrative, then you begin to hear a new, kinder and compassionate voice.

BRAIN TRAINING EXERCISE: NAME IT TO TAME IT

This is one of my favourite exercises by psychiatrist Dr. Daniel Siegel. When you experience a negative emotion (sadness, jealousy, anger, etc.), sit down and write out the feeling. Then write out how that negative emotion feels in your body. Sit with this information, even if it's uncomfortable. Allow yourself to embrace it so then you can allow it to pass. When you recognize the emotion, your brain steps into problem-solving mode and releases soothing neurotransmitters to stabilize your mindset and bodyset. In this moment, you create a new memory and will recognize that the discomfort was tolerable. Reminder: there are no good or bad emotions, there is being human and how we choose to interpret the emotions. When you start to process your emotions, it becomes easier to step away from your numbing behaviours because you no longer avoid what your inner critic is saying and what emotions follow suit.

CHAPTER 11

BOUNDARIES

Being a top-notch people pleaser meant I had zero boundaries or a lack thereof. I didn't realize how bad my boundaries were because I didn't even realize boundaries were a thing. What I now know is that when you don't have boundaries established, you can slip into burnout quite easily and become jealous of the women around you who have boundaries in place.

Again, society and culture pit women against each other; one way this happens is when a woman sets a boundary that fits her lifestyle, while another woman thinks she can't set the same boundary because she isn't worth it or her inner critic said so. I fell victim to this more often than not.

Even recently, I got off the phone with a client, Nicole, who said she was so pissed at another colleague who recently started at her office. This newest member didn't have to work Saturdays. Nicole was livid because she put in all these years of work with the company and still had to work Saturdays.

I asked, "When you first started, did you ask for Saturdays off?"

Nicole replied, "No, I took whatever they gave me and was happy with it."

"Did you want Saturdays off?"

"Ya, I did."

"Do you want Saturdays off now?"

"I do!"

"What if you asked for Saturdays off?"

Naturally, this cause Nicole to think. She was initially pissed that this new person starting didn't have to work Saturdays. What I showed Nicole was that she wasn't mad at this new younger woman who started. Instead, she was upset she didn't realize she could ask for Saturdays off. I offered Nicole a different perspective that made her a priority where she could set boundaries and ask for what she wanted.

I want you to start to think about how you view other women and question why competition exists. I even want you to think about how you peruse social media or show up in conversations with others and think, "Must be nice." That sentence is jealousy at its core and it's because you don't think you can set your own boundaries. But I am here to show you how setting boundaries is important to navigate and how to set your inner critic straight.

A boundary, physical or psychological, is a limit you put in place to protect your time, energy, and mental space. Think of it as drawing a line in the sand and determining what you allow to cross. Boundaries are necessary for the high achiever, especially for those who experience impostor phenomenon (IP), perfectionism, and people pleasing. Boundaries allow you to determine what in your life is a *negotiable* or a *non-negotiable. Non-negotiables* are people (including yourself), holidays and events, vacations, and self-care that you deem top priorities. You make the time, energy, and space for them. These things should go at the top of your list, and they get put into your calendar first. The *negotiables* are the things that come up that aren't as important or don't take priority. These are the things you can and should say "no" to. Once your non-negotiables are on the calendar, then the negotiables fit in accordingly.

Boundaries are both physical and psychological because of the link we create in our minds. They can be solely mantras or intentions around your beliefs and values, or they can be tangible actions that signify a separation between two entities, for example, a boundary between work and home life. Sometimes it's hard to create that separation and leave work at work. One way I have my clients input a separation between work and home is to link a habit and a mantra to the end of their workday. That could be the moment they lock their car and say, "My work today is done." Or it could be getting home, taking a step into the shower, and saying, "I am washing away the work, whether good or bad, from today. Work is done."

This takes practice, and you may not hardwire it in on the first go. Maybe for you it's hanging up your keys when you get home, emptying your water bottle, or changing into comfy clothes. Whatever you decide works for you, stick with it for no less than four to six weeks (*Atomic Habits* by James Clear is a great resource to explore in-depth habit creation and dismantling). The longer you stick with it, the better, because it takes time for your mindset and bodyset to adjust to new habits.

Boundaries also come in the form of limits around your time and people. These can be challenging if you're a high-achieving perfectionist and people pleaser, because you feel the need to do more. It is truly asking yourself what you want to do, how you want to spend your time, and who you want to spend your time with. The high achiever can have a hard time saying "no" because they fear they won't get asked again. There is such a thing as over-extending yourself and reaching a point of burnout because you didn't have adequate boundaries in place. A client of mine uses an affirmation that I love, "Boundaries make me a better mother, daughter, sister, friend, and boss!"

There were months when I didn't take time for breaks. If someone or something needed me, I jumped at the opportunity to help. I always said "yes," especially when it came to my career and family, even when I didn't have the time or energy. Running on fumes seemed normal, and those fumes kept me in survival mode.

Research suggests that saying "yes" too often at work can lead to diminished quality of work, overstretched resources, and feeling overwhelmed.[39] At this point, your inner critic convinces you that if you don't say "yes," then you'll be missing out and won't be able to get ahead. But the flip side is, if you don't rest, there won't be any of you left to get ahead. If you fear losing out on an opportunity at work or that your boss won't ask you again, then here are some responses you can include in your toolbox of saying "no":

RESPONSES FOR SAYING "NO" WHEN YOU WANT TO SAY "YES": WORK EDITION

The Response	The Intent
"No, not now."	Finite and straightforward. Gives the person asking information that maybe in the future you would want to be asked again.
"I'm unavailable at this time, but would definitely like to be asked again."	Indirectly saying no and letting the person asking know you want to be asked again.
"Thanks for thinking of me, but I don't have the capacity right now."	Offering appreciation is something I like when you want to thank the person who asked. If you aren't appreciative (and that's totally fine), you do not need to thank them. Also, this gives information that you are busy and don't have time.

The Response	The Intent
"I want to say yes, but at the present, my time is being directed elsewhere."	Sharing with the asking person that you would like to help, but you don't have the time, energy, or space presently to give to them.
"Thanks for asking, but that is a fast-approaching deadline and I don't have the time to meet it."	Offering appreciation but indicating to the person who asked that if the deadline was further away then you might have been able to help. This sets a boundary of providing information to the asking person that you require time in order to help.
"Let me think on it and get back to you by XX date."	This is one of my favourites because you are asking for time back. You don't have to feel pressured to make an immediate decision. By responding this way, you give yourself the opportunity to ponder what you want. I also appreciate when people let me know when they will get back to me because then I'm not breathing down their neck wondering what they will say. This situation helps both parties.

Remember, you don't need to feel guilty for implementing a boundary to protect your time, energy, and mental space. You also don't need to justify your response. Women, in general, have been conditioned to explain a reason for their answer. "No" is a complete sentence. If you don't feel comfortable outright saying "no," then you can start by using the responses in the table to see what works and sits well with you.

Just know that when you choose to implement these new responses, the first few times you try them you are likely going to think the dead air that lingers, that silence, is excruciatingly painful. The only person who thinks it's painful is you. The other person likely isn't feeling or thinking the same thing. That's your inner critic convincing you the discomfort you feel by setting a boundary and stepping into the silence is bad. It's not bad, it's new and different.

The more you choose to set boundaries and practice saying "no," the easier it will be. Eventually that silence will feel different and your inner critic won't be telling you, "They think you're lying," or "They did you a favour, you should be doing them a favour, too," or "You're never going to get asked again." Lastly, do not apologize during that silence or when you respond with a "no." You have nothing to be sorry about, because you know your non-negotiables.

Let's talk about time, energy, and boundaries. Similar to what we talked about in Part I, Impostor Phenomenon, implementing time blocks helps to prevent overworking and avoidance. When you implement boundaries, you give yourself time and energy back because you aren't giving them to people, tasks, projects, or events you don't want to be giving to. This includes friends and family as well. An important boundary is the one you need to protect your mental and physical space so you can take care of yourself. You can't take care of others if you are constantly sacrificing yourself. The moment you say, "I'm overwhelmed and don't have time for me" is the same moment you say, "I've made the choice that I'm not a priority." Time is a choice. If you don't like how you're spending it, you can choose differently. If you keep saying "yes" no matter what, then you are also saying "no" to things you really want to be doing, neglecting your own needs in the process.

RESPONSES FOR SAYING "NO" WHEN YOU WANT TO SAY "YES": FAMILY AND FRIENDS EDITION

The Response	The Intent
"Thaaaanks so much for the invite and I would love to be invited again, but I have something else going on (or, I'm not free)."	Be gentle, kind, but firm with friends. Same holds true with how much you choose to share. You never have to justify or over-explain. I do think it is courtesy at times to share the concept of why, although you do not need to go into details, especially if friends keep asking you and you keep saying no but you still want them to ask you in the future; context is important.
"Oh snap, I won't be able to make that, but what if we did XX instead?"	You can fill in the blanks accordingly, (and you don't need to start with "oh snap"). What I like about this is you propose another option. That way it doesn't feel like you're bailing. You aren't bailing, but sometimes that's what we feel like we are doing.

Do not respond by saying, "Sorry, I can't," because you likely aren't sorry, and you likely can but you don't want to. That's a big difference. Your choice of words in these situations will give your inner critic ammunition to seek out why you should feel guilty. You care for the people around you whether it is friends, family, colleagues, clients, or even people on the street. If you are reading this, you likely struggle with caring too much at times so it becomes hard to create boundaries. It feels as if you are constantly being hurt because you care too much.

When I described burnout before, I talked about the component of cynicism and compassion fatigue. For the lot of you who care immensely, you may resonate with the term *empath.*

Empathy is "the ability to imagine and understand the thoughts, perspective, and emotions of another person."[40] An empath takes it one step further and is highly attuned to the people around them and can actually take on those feelings, whether it is family, friends, your partner, colleagues, or someone you are meeting for the first time. For the high achiever and people pleaser, experiencing empathy means it is difficult to set boundaries because you care and can put yourself in someone else's shoes. It becomes easier to bend your boundaries to accommodate someone else's needs and mood.

A lot of women develop this skill based on past experiences from childhood, not just by being a high achiever. If you lived in a household with an unpredictable adult—someone who had mental illness or was angry or narcissistic—then you had to be attuned to them in order to protect yourself. You likely even developed behaviours so you could "smooth things over" or "make someone else feel better." Is this starting to sound familiar? Like in Part III, People Pleasing? Because that's exactly what it is. Let me remind you, it is not your job to make someone happy. It is the other person's responsibility to make themselves happy, and it is your responsibility to make yourself happy. You control your inner voice, emotions, reactions, behaviours, thoughts, and boundaries.

If you experienced an unpredictable adult from an early age, then your FF response was constantly activated, adding to your overall nervous system dysregulation and affecting how you experience burnout. From my calculation, if it's been years that your nervous system has been out of whack, one glamorous vacation or spa day is not going to fix burnout overnight.

If you are someone who relates better with anxious or nervous individuals or feels for someone you meet for the first time, it's because you know exactly what it feels like but you also know how to shift that person's mood. To me, that isn't an empath, that is a spectacular *observer.* This is why when you walk into a room, you can recognize and feel the person who is tense. Your nervous system has been programmed to recognize their stress and be on guard, which is when your FF response is activated. Being on guard means your subconscious feels unsafe and you become ready to jump in when necessary. For the high-achieving-people-pleaser-perfectionist-observer, this is why it is hard to enter a room and feel joy immediately. Your internal program has been primed to react out of fear of uncertainty instead of potential calmness, ease, and comfort. I didn't start connecting the dots for this until I heard Brené Brown share one of her experiences and I thought, "Woah, why is no one talking more about this?" As an aside, shout out to Brené for breaking down emotions so we can learn more about them.

To help with this, you can create boundaries around how you want to experience your emotions and empathy. You have to actively practice this, but it is possible. For example, let's say you are getting ready to walk into a board meeting and previously you used to subconsciously scan the room to see if anyone was pissed so you could predict how the meeting would go. Try walking into that meeting next time with a boundary around scanning the room, and only manage how your emotions show up. Instead of looking for the person who is pissed, look for the person who is inquisitive or amused. Sometimes boundaries are with yourself and sometimes they involve other people. You can choose whose burden you are willing to take on.

When you care a lot, it can be difficult to set and stick to boundaries, especially when you first implement them. If your boundaries are challenged, know this is not a reflection of who you are as an individual. It is a reflection of how that other individual perceives the boundary you implemented. **You can't and won't make everyone happy, so why not make yourself happy?**

When high-achieving women are overextended and burnt out, they can become resentful and envious toward other women, thereby thinking they are competition. Let's talk about women's power in our culture and society. For as long as I can remember, any woman I looked at was considered competition, whether it was in looks, brains, or strength. Constantly comparing myself to others meant I was already behind before I even started. Comparing myself to others led to delusions of who I ought to be. That was not healthy. When I was in the pit of my burnout, in that deep, dark abyss, I was angry at the women around me. My competition had it all together; she was beautiful, successful, strong, and bought a house. If I helped them, which, let's be real, I always did, I would come home angry for helping them. They were going to get ahead, and I was going to stay stuck. I mentioned this earlier as well, but I truly believe our society keeps women in competition with each other because they understand how powerful we are as a community. Because I cared so much and bit off more than I could chew (no dental pun intended), that anger toward other women was actually envy and resentment that they felt comfortable asking me for help, something I could never do myself. Asking for help and implementing boundaries meant I wasn't strong enough to do it all. What *all* meant, I had no clue. But I was determined to do it *all*, regardless.

In *Atlas of the Heart*, by Brené Brown, she shares this enlightening component: that resentment and jealousy aren't in the anger family of emotions, but instead in the envious family. I didn't want exactly what that other woman had; I was envious that she had better boundaries than I did. She knew how to utilize her time and energy, so she wasn't depleted at the end of the day, sitting like a blob in front of the TV. When I recognized this difference, I started implementing boundaries everywhere. Family got boundaries, friends got boundaries, patients got boundaries, employees got boundaries, men got boundaries, everyone got boundaries. It took a long time to be okay with these new boundaries; people who weren't used to it would push back, which initially I caved into. I couldn't say "no" to family and friends because that meant trying a new way of doing things, and my inner critic had gotten me to the point where I was today, a high achiever with multiple accolades. Albeit, I was unhappy and burnt out. Each day I chose not to implement or stick to a boundary was another day longer it would take to heal. And I was no longer willing to accept me as a negotiable because I was tired of waking up scared every morning, thinking I wasn't enough.

Creating boundaries, both psychological and physical, protects your time, energy, and mental space. When I implemented boundaries, the people who got my time and energy got me at 100 percent instead of everyone and everything only getting 50 percent. Not everyone deserves your time and energy, but your inner critic devalues your worth. The day you choose to listen to your inner cheerleader is the day you decide you are worthy and take back control of your boundaries.

CHAPTER 12

REST FOR THE WEARY

Being productive is both working toward and achieving a goal, but it is also *active rest.* Sleeping, resting, exercise, reading, journaling, meditating, breathing, enjoying your hobbies, or sitting intentionally in front of the TV are all forms of active rest, which is considered productive time. In the twenty-first century, productive time has been mislabeled as time when you go-go-go. The high-achieving woman can confuse rest and play as stupid, lazy, and unnecessary. This is why when I was burnt out, I often worked six to seven days a week. There were months when I had only two days off. I looked at the people around me, at the money they made, and how they worked, and I thought I had to grind and hustle to get to that stage.

I thought productive time was equivalent to what society deems the "grind and hustle." If you weren't grinding and hustling, or starting a side gig, then you were wasting your time as a high achiever. For me, additional pressure came in regards to my career as a single, unmarried high-achieving woman. Since I didn't have kids, then I should be the one staying late at work and covering holidays. For a mother, society's standards shifted slightly and "allowed" her to leave work on time so she could attend her next full-time job of raising a family and maintaining a household. As I wrote that sentence, I almost vomited in my mouth. The social climate of today is still ass-backwards. Yes, we have taken strides in feminism but there is still a lot of responsibility placed on mothers to be super humans and maintain the same level of energy both at work and at home.

There was no coincidence when I stumbled onto the Instagram account @themamaattorney when I wrote this section. Similar to the stance of the former Associate Justice of the United States Supreme Court Ruth Bader Ginsburg, fighting for women's rights means one must also advocate for men's rights, which bring all genders together as fighting for human rights. @ themamattorney, Daphne Delvaux, wrote, "Even women without kids get punished under the motherhood tax. An assumption is made that she may become pregnant and take time off work so it's better to exclude her from positions and promotions preemptively. The solution? Men must take time off for caregiving in equal measure." This is a different perspective that would not only strengthen the role of caregiver for men, but give women the opportunity to listen to her mindset and bodyset. I'm done blaming my body for failing me in moments I can't control due to being a woman. And I can't be the high achiever I want to be if I don't choose to rest and take care of myself.

Now at this point, I'm going to take us back to the two massive unrealistic and dated expectations around time and energy for women: mothers need to be super humans on the home front *and* work front. They get to leave on time but are still expected to move at the same rate as they worked before they had kids. Women who are single are expected to be super humans by putting in overtime and working through holidays because they are childless. Either way, whether a parent or childless, women are expected to stay late to "prove" themselves.

What about this radical thought: how about no one stays late and companies put reasonable expectations on their employees with appropriate time-dependent deadlines? No one, I mean no one, should be in the hustle and grind. The same holds true if you own your own business or are CEO. Consider setting realistic expectations for yourself as a leader.

I dislike the term "hustle and grind," because the impostor phenomenon (IP) perfectionist high achiever can take this to the extreme. It can definitely keep you focused and on task, but it can also make you feel scattered, depleted, and lacking. Instead, finding a balance that works for you is important. If you can change your belief around what "working hard" means and incorporating time to take care of yourself through active rest, then you get to be the high achiever you want to be that doesn't feel overwhelmed, exhausted, and inadequate.

This misconception and misinformation around unrealistic expectations and the lack of boundaries kept me in burnout because I didn't think I was allowed, as per society's standards, to enjoy my free time. No wonder women are pitted against each other. Regardless the stage of life a woman is in, the number of pressures placed on her are unrealistic and unattainable. No one can live up to these pressures and still remain happy, fulfilled, joyful, powerful and hopeful in all aspects of their lives.

Similar to how IP beliefs were instilled, cognitive dissonance reigns true across many aspects of how women are supposed to think, feel, and act. In this book, I hope to show you a different perspective. For the single women or women who are childless, look at your friends who are mothers through a different lens; and for women with kids, look at your friends who are single or childless through a different lens. If together we aspire to build a community on a foundation of support, vulnerability, and collaboration, then we no longer would see each other as competition.

To tie this in with our previous chapter, this is why boundaries for women at all stages of life are important. If you put boundaries in place, not only are you protecting your time, energy and mental space, but you are creating an environment where you no longer resent or envy your fellow strong woman Your inner critic stops pitting you against others. Booya!

We briefly touched on productive time so I want us to go back and explore it a bit further. When I was putting myself back together, piece by piece, there were a flurry of questions at any given time when I rested. *Why can't you be productive all the time? Why do you have to rest and take down time? Why do you need to sleep? Why are you so lazy?* I blamed getting older and claimed my body was failing me. I wanted to do it all but I couldn't because I didn't have the energy. A large portion of not having enough energy was because I overextended myself, spent time stewing while in avoidance, and stayed anxious. It all related back to experiencing the impostor cycle and how I viewed me.

Below, you'll see I have added another cycle to the already existing impostor and perfectionism cycle. You will now see the anxiety cycle. Whether you procrastinate or overwork, a short-term relief is engaging in numbing behaviour. Over time, the temporary relief adds up, creating a long-term effect that can come with chronic illnesses. This ultimately affects your resilience and ability to cope with stressors. Regardless, whether you over-worked or avoided, the task or goal still needs to get done and this comes with increased anxiety. When you stay stuck in this cycle, repeating the same patterns and behaviours keeps you in the FF response; constantly scanning for perceived danger. This is living in survival mode, feeling like you're waiting for the shoe to drop, or having your guard up. Take a look below.

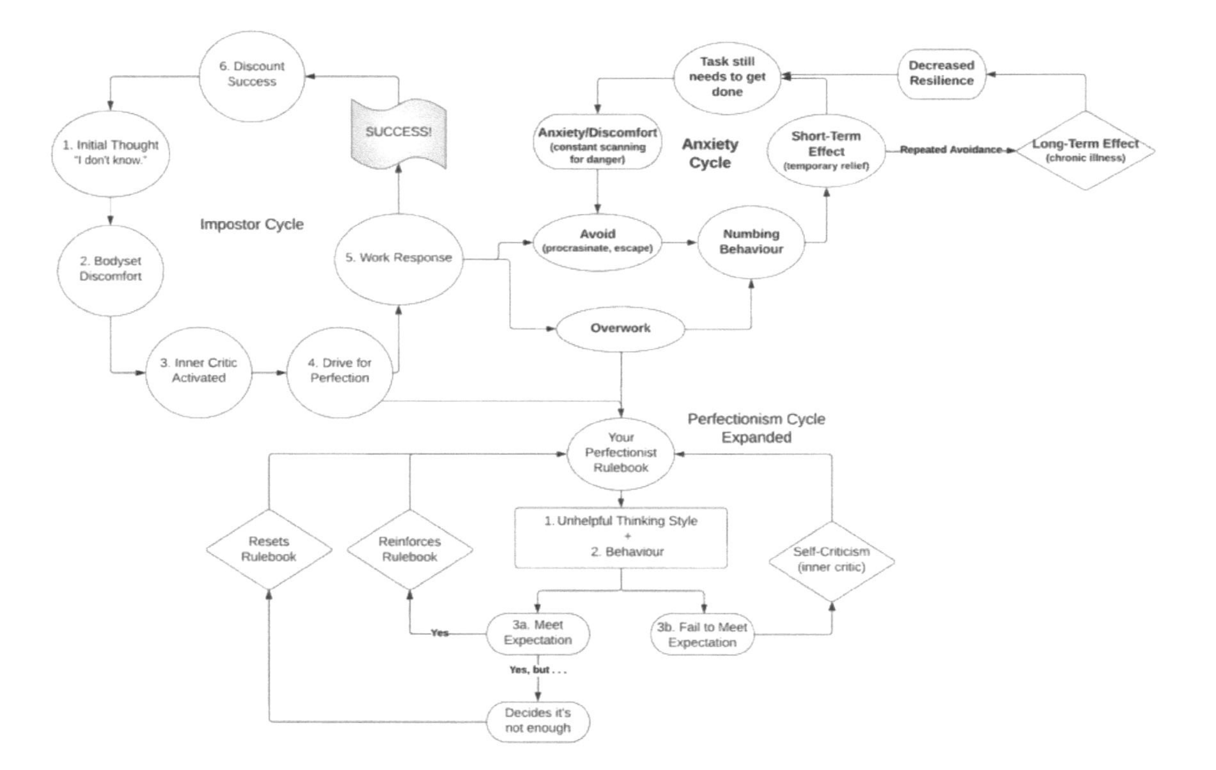

Mind Map: Impostor Cycle + Perfectionism Cycle Expanded + Anxiety Cycle

The American Psychological Association describes resilience "as the process of adapting well in the face of adversity, trauma, tragedy, threats, or significant sources of stress—such as family and relationship problems, serious health problems, or workplace and financial stressors."[41] [42] It is both "bouncing back" from challenging circumstances and your own personal growth that allows you to be resilient. When I start to reflect on why I didn't have time, energy, or mental capacity to manage my anxiety, it wasn't because I was doing all the wrong things, but because I wasn't meeting my needs or making time for the things I wanted to be doing. My priorities, my non-negotiables, and my boundaries were nonexistent. The one constant that remained annoyingly loud was, *You don't have the strength to be resilient,* as said by my inner critic.

Now you may not be able to control your FF response because it does have an autopilot, your sympathetic nervous system. However, you can control your parasympathetic nervous system, which is the "rest-and-digest" response (RD). RD response complements the FF response by helping your body relax. It helps slow your heart rate, lowers your blood pressure, and promotes digestion. I bet you're wondering, "This sounds wonderful Jessica, but I can't control how my body responds." Well, I'm here to tell you that you do have some control. You can activate your RD response through its great and powerful on-switch: breathing. You can't directly control how fast your heart is beating but you can indirectly control your heart rate by controlling your breathing. This is why there are courses, workshops, and retreats dedicated to teaching you belly breathing and breathwork.

Earlier in the book, I suggested trying the 333 rule to bring you back to the present time (3.2 Bodyset). You can add on breathwork to this exercise or you can harness your breath on its own. Controlled breathing, deep breathing, diaphragmatic breathing and belly breathing activate your RD response and help calm the FF response. When you thought you had no control over how your bodyset responds, remember you do. I'm going to walk you through two different styles of breathwork I use. Harnessing your breath can feel very powerful when you practice often. When you can control how your bodyset responds, you control what connection gets created with your inner cheerleader. Just like anything, it will take time for you to absolutely master it.

BRAIN TRAINING EXERCISE: BREATHWORK

1. Exhale longer than you inhale. Inhale for a count of five, hold for a count of two, exhale for a count of seven, and hold for a count of two. This is really hard initially when you experience your FF response. If you have difficulty getting to seven, start to hum. It extends the life of the breath.
2. Box Breathing. Inhale for a count of four, hold for a count of four, exhale for a count of four, hold for a count of four.

Try either one and figure out which one you like better. You may even notice that you prefer one over the other based on the FF response you experience.

All Rey wanted to do after work was sit on the couch and watch TV while she snuggled with her pup. As she sat, her husband worked on renovating the office. Baseboards were stripped, wallpaper removed, and carpet uplifted.

Even on Sunday afternoons, she took time with her dog and enjoyed a good TV show while her husband did construction. As Rey sat there, she couldn't enjoy her TV show. She felt like she was "wasting" time and she should be more productive.

Men and women are built differently, as are introverts and extroverts. Some people need alone time to replenish their energy, and some people need to be around others to replenish their energy. Some people need to be fixing and doing to replenish their energy, and some people need to be sitting in nature, reading a book, or watching TV. We each have different styles of productive time. Rest, relaxation, recovery, and play are all forms of productive time, and implementing boundaries around this time is just as important as the boundaries you put around errands, getting to-do lists done, or achieving.

It's easy for us to see when an athlete needs to recover, it is light training or no training. But when a high achiever needs to recover, we only deem it as sleep. But all productive time is time well spent. The tough part is trying to get over the guilt that comes with it. Rey and I worked on how she viewed her productive time. We changed the vocabulary she used. Productive time was rest and relaxation, which to her was alone time with her dog and one of her favourite TV shows, even while her husband worked in the background.

Rey told me that her husband viewed productivity as always doing something, renovating the house, going out with friends, and being with family.

I asked Rey, "But aren't you doing something when you are watching TV? Aren't you productively reenergizing yourself?" It was always easier to sit in front of the TV when her husband left the house because it took the pressure off how she chose to rest. As soon as her husband came home, she felt like she couldn't watch TV anymore because he had told her it was wasted time. I helped Rey bring up this difficult conversation with her husband around her needs, and helped her change her perspective around her definition of rest. By stepping into this challenge, Rey noticed she felt less guilty when she reframed wasted time to actively resting. She also observed she was less irritated with work and her husband. To me, this was a win-win because Rey gave herself the permission to let her inner cheerleader reframe her perception of active rest.

When you slowly start to change your critic to cheerleader,

kinder words may seem insincere at first. Similar to starting to navigate your FF response, regulating a dysregulated nervous system can feel bizarre. As you navigate through having more time and energy, you may start to feel bored. Boredom when you are on the journey of healing shouldn't be framed as disinterest or impatience due to restlessness. Boredom should be reframed as an opportunity to feel hopeful, content, and peaceful. Peace is confused as boredom for the high achievers and perfectionists because they are constantly afraid of their future while also regretting the past. **It is in boredom you are giving yourself the opportunity to find rest, relaxation, play, and creativity.**

When I was only *doing*, I stopped dreaming and became jaded. Going through the motions isn't enough to get to an end result. Once I allowed myself the opportunity to dream and be creative, I gave myself the permission, as the high achiever, to rewrite my story and narrative.

BRAIN TRAINING EXERCISE: DEFINING ACTIVE REST

1) When you have downtime, how do you spend that time?
    - Do you see those activities as beneficial? Why or why not?
    - If not, ponder this: do those activities fill your energy tank? Do you feel more whole or rested afterwards?
2) What is your definition of rest?
    - Do you see rest as beneficial? Why or why not?
    - If not, ponder this: what does it feel like when you haven't rested? Check in with yourself mentally, emotionally, and physically. How does your mind feel without rest? Do you notice your emotions are amplified or heightened? What symptoms present in your bodyset?

CHAPTER 13

CREATING HEALTHY HABITS

Moving through burnout and coming out the other side is not as glamorous as social media and North American culture make it out to be. It is downright dirty. There are days when things go well and it's as if the stars and sun have aligned, and then there are days when it feels as if everything went wrong. However, each day you decide to make a change is another day of burnout recovery and healing. Be patient and kind with yourself, because amplifying your inner cheerleader is not an easy feat, albeit totally worth it. You are worth it. That's why I'm taking the time to discuss self-care, healthy habits, and prioritizing you.

Up until now in Part III, I have explained the difference between burnout, anxiety, stress and worry. I've taken you through the anxiety cycle, which is an add-on to the impostor cycle, and I've broken down what happens when you choose to overwork or avoid from a short- and long-term perspective. Numbing behaviours and implementing boundaries were described in detail as well, and finally I shared reframing active rest. **All of these things add up to one specific element for me: how we choose to speak to ourselves so we know we are worthy of meeting both our needs and wants.**

Now, let's start by talking about our gas tank of motivation and energy (ME). Most days you wake up with a full tank. If you didn't get enough sleep or you tossed and turned, the tank may only be half full (sometimes it may even be less than that). It is on those days you need to be extra kind to yourself and recognize decision-making might not come as easily; you may move slower, and you may experience more emotions. That's totally normal. Give yourself the permission to move through this day with a different expectation.

On days when I didn't get enough sleep the night before, I usually start my day by saying, "I'm curious how today will unfold." Right there, it takes the pressure off. If instead I wake up saying, "Today has to go great," and it doesn't go great, then the whole day becomes a shitshow. If I wake up and say, "Well crap, today is going to be a crap day," then my mindset will pick up on all the little things that go wrong, and because I'm tired, my negative emotions will be amplified.

In both of these situations, you've already set your expectation to a level where you will be disappointed before the day even begins, or regardless of how it ends. Being "curious" sets the stage for you to experience whatever presents itself with an open mind so you don't get stuck in an expectation. Remember, words matter and have meaning.

Going back to your motivation and energy (ME) gas tank: let me describe what happens throughout any given day. Whether you start with a full or half tank of motivation and energy, by the end of the day the gas tank is lower. On most days, it is hypothesized that you make close to 35,000 decisions each day.[43] Of course you are going to be tired; your brain is a problem-solving machine, and that is why it is easy to slip into numbing behaviours at the end of the day. As a human being, you want to make yourself feel better, but if you expend more energy ruminating, avoiding, or partaking in numbing behaviours, then you are depleting your ME gas tank instead of filling it. Healthy habits and speaking kindly to yourself help replenish it.

Here are additional ways to keep your ME gas tank full or at a sustainable level. One way is to do the tasks that are most challenging, time-consuming, or energy-depleting in the part of the day when you have the most energy. If you are a morning person, that would be the first half of the day, and if you are an evening person that may be the latter half. That way you don't have to muster the willpower when you are tired. Willpower alone doesn't create healthy habits. For example, this is why you may find yourself eating healthy all day, only to binge on chocolate and ice cream at night because you've used all the willpower, motivation, and energy throughout the day. Read this carefully: you don't go back to old eating habits at the end of a day because you're not capable of stepping into new healthy habits, it's because you resort back to what makes you feel good and comfortable when your ME gas tank is low. Your FF response wants to be deactivated; eating unhealthily soothes you for the time being.

Okay, I totally got specific with one habit around eating, but this applies to watching TV into the wee hours of the night, having an alcoholic beverage, avoiding meaningful conversations with your partner, and much more. That comfort that comes from the numbing behaviour helps soothe you from how the day unfolded. However, you can choose to nourish yourself differently. Creating new habits will start to soothe you as well, but you have to give it time to work and view these habits as nourishing.

Think of creating new habits as running a marathon. Up until now, you may have been a sprinter, getting to the end really fast and knowing that the end is in sight even at the starting line. But a marathon is harder. You can't see the finish line at the start. This would be a great time for you to see that your inner cheerleader is with you along the way. They may not be running next to you, because maybe they are on that golf cart cheering you on, passing you cups of water, playing your favourite music and saying you most definitely are capable. Kudos to my friend the soon-to-be author Courtney Herring for this analogy.

Whether you're a morning person or a night person, you can

create nourishing habits that soothe you based on what works for you. This is why the book *The 5am Club* works for certain individuals; get everything strenuous out of the way earlier in the day like journaling, exercising, and personal growth. The concept is that if someone doesn't want to do these things, they should stack them first thing in the morning. However, what isn't acknowledged in this book is that not everyone's physiological clock allows them to wake up at five o'clock. It also doesn't allow people to do journaling, exercising, or personal growth during other parts of their day if that works best for them and their schedule. Some women's bodies' schedules and individual circadian rhythms don't allow them to wake up at five o'clock. Therefore, it's unreasonable to set that expectation. I remember having a conversation with one of my personal trainers years ago when she read *The 5am Club*. She was so distraught when she told me she would never be able to live at her truest potential because she just couldn't get up at five o'clock. I asked her, "What is your usual wake-up time?"

She hesitated. "Ten o'clock."

"What if you applied the same techniques from five o'clock and started them at ten o'clock?"

I saw her facial expression change from being perplexed to inspired. All I did was give her the opportunity to see a different perspective. In doing this, instead of beating herself up and having her inner critic tell her she won't ever be good enough, her inner cheerleader now had the opportunity to step in and show her the way.

On days where you feel like your ME tank is at 2 percent, it's important to set realistic expectations and treat yourself with compassion if you aren't capable of doing all you would usually do. However, the 2 percent days can also be the game time days, the days where you bring in all the activities that replenish your ME tank that you practiced.

Let's say you play rugby. You practice and train for a game. For the love of all good things, if you showed up to a rugby game without practice you would likely injure yourself and never want to play again. Same holds true for rewiring your brain; think of the rugby game as a shit day. If you just showed up on a shit day expecting to implement mantras, change your narrative, and speak kindly to yourself for the first time, you would never believe it. You have to practice, rewire, and brain train.

Whether you had a good day or a bad day, you should find a moment to reflect instead of just going through the motions. It is really easy to just move on to the next day if everything went well instead of embracing the good. And it's just as easy to stay stuck on a shit day. So why not recall a good day and examine why it was good? Below is a brain training exercise to get you started.

BRAIN TRAINING EXERCISE: CROSS-EXAMINING A GOOD DAY AND A BAD DAY

	Good Day of Work	**Bad Day of Work**
What went bad?	There was an unplanned, last minute performance review.	My colleague bombarded me with issues before being able to take my jacket off and settle in to work.
What went well?	I was told I am doing great at work and to keep it up.	I didn't react and become frantic like I usually would.

	Good Day of Work	Bad Day of Work
What did I learn?	Not all unplanned meetings are going to be negative. I didn't immediately jump to catastrophizing and reframed how I viewed my current performance. I went into the meeting taking an observer role instead of jumping in defensive.	I will speak with my colleague and share how I would like to be communicated to. I will kindly ask her to inform me when there are concerns and she would like to speak to me when settled.

To set this up for yourself, you can write it down or you can reflect on it in your mind. No matter if you had a good day or a bad day, ask yourself these three questions: What went bad? What went well? What did I learn? These questions allow you to find positives and negatives on both days. On a good day, when you ask yourself the question "what went well," you can then find repeatable patterns to replicate good days. Maybe you had coffee with a friend mid-morning on a Monday, or your staff managed a specific problem you can now delegate, or you time-blocked multiple meetings. A key component to comparing and contrasting is finding the necessary evidence that reminds you that you are capable, skillful, qualified, and have experience to step into being a confident high achiever.

As an aside, I really like doing this exercise when I'm on vacation. It's so fun! The bad is usually not that bad, and the good is good. Can you have an off day on vacation? Totally, but it gives you the opportunity to search your mind and find stand-out moments and commit them to memory. On my most recent vacation, the bad thing that happened was that my sandwich got wet while I was on a boat, which isn't bad at all because I was on a boat in the open ocean. The good thing that happened was the crescent moon I got to see by getting up really early to drive to the boat adventure. And I learned that looking up at the sky can really change my mood for the good. Not only do I do this exercise with myself, but I include the people around me so I hear their thoughts as well.

Another way to keep your ME gas tank sustainable is to practice time-blocking active rest and self-care throughout the day, week, and month. It's time to get yourself out of the cycle of burning the candle at both ends and waiting until the weekend or a vacation to crash. In a day, that may mean you carve out time for lunch instead of working through lunch. In a week, that may mean you carve out dedicated time to hang out with friends or make sure you get to sleep on time. In a month, that may look like a weekend when you have a boundary and no plans are scheduled. You have options!

Implementing a self-care regimen is something I teach all of my clients to do, recognizing that over time it might change based on their needs and wants. Again, if my clients go in "curious" about building a self-care regimen, it becomes a creative experiment instead of a forced routine.

Over the span of a few months, I worked with Rey on implementing her boundaries and holding firm to them, because boundaries are a part of self-care and protecting your mental space. As discussed above, we already knew that Rey and her husband worked on different wavelengths when it came to defining productive rest time, which meant their self-care regimens would be different as well . . . and that's okay! Together, we examined different combinations that allowed Rey to ask herself what self-care, self-love, and her wants really were. You can do the same with the brain training exercise below.

BRAIN TRAINING EXERCISE: SELF-CARE CREATIVE EXPERIMENT

I have found there to be five pillars of self-care. You will have to do some experimenting and figure out what works best for you. Just like any experiment, there is a hypothesis, data gathering, results, statistical analysis, and then a discussion on whether you accept or reject the hypothesis. That's what you get to do here with this self-care creative experiment.

1. **Physical Care.** What do you need to take care of your bodyset? How do you want to move your body? Examples: weightlifting, dance, walking, hiking? What do you need to feed yourself that nourishes your body? How much sleep do you need not just to function, but to be rested?
2. **Emotional Care.** If you are experiencing challenging emotions, how would you like to spend time processing them? Alone time? Calling your trust squad (discussed in Part IV)? Maybe a bit of both? How will you choose to embrace all emotions?
3. **Mental Care.** What do you need to take care of your mindset? Does writing or journaling help organize your thoughts so they don't appear disordered or chaotic? When you feel overwhelmed, what helps calm your mind? What is your definition of success and happiness?
4. **Spiritual Care.** Regardless of your belief, what do you need for your spirit and soul? Is it prayer or meditation? Is it nature, yoga, or church? Or is it something I haven't even listed here? I've had my own challenges with this pillar because I was raised Catholic but no longer go to church and don't identify with Catholicism. Now, I am way more spiritual and connected to nature.

5. **Community Care.** Whether you are an introvert or an extrovert, it's good to know how much interaction you want from others. How much time do you want to spend with family, friends, or coworkers? What social environments or interactions pull from your ME tank and deplete you? Who are the people in your life that replenish your ME tank and share in your successes?

As a reminder, once you have done all the self-care and have implemented it for a period of time, if you notice something still isn't working, look externally to your environment and examine what is going on at work or in your personal life. At that point, it doesn't matter how much self-care you practice; something is no longer working and needs to be adjusted. This isn't a "you" problem, but rather an environment problem.

When Rey is stuck in a negative emotion, likely due to work, she knows she needs time to process, and, as much as she loves her husband and venting to him, she also needs alone time. On one of our calls, she described to me childhood memories of stepping away from her family to go to her bedroom, close the door, lie on her bed, and stare at the ceiling. During those moments of solitude, she would ponder her thoughts and recoup her energy. When ready, she would head back out to be with her family. Rey now communicates this to her partner so he doesn't feel like she is avoiding him or pissed at him. **In this way, healthy habits are linked to boundaries because it is important to implement boundaries around your healthy habits and self-care.**

Along with her alone time, Rey recognizes she sometimes likes to call up a friend, make a new recipe, get a facial, and go for a thirty-minute walk with her dog. Practicing self-care over time creates consistency. The way I like to think of consistency is reflected in the micro-progress steps you may not see. If you had a goal at the top of a staircase, then each step toward that goal is progress. Sometimes you take a step up and see the growth, and sometimes you take a step back because something didn't work or you learned something different. In moments when you feel like you've fallen off a step or you're being triggered by something you feel like you've already healed, I'm offering a change in perspective. Drifting down a step is not falling backwards and regressing. Use this time as an opportunity to reflect on why you are being triggered. The trigger likely was activated so you could do more processing and healing.

There were times along my journey—and yes, it still happens from time to time—when my triggers are activated and I get so frustrated with myself. *Why is this bothering me again? I already did the work on this!* Instead of getting angry, critical, and irritated with myself, I began to ask, *What more can I learn from this? How can I see this as an opportunity instead of a problem?* The reframing allowed me to be curious, just as we have talked about before around expectations. Instead of thinking I fell down a step, I thought of it as drifting through a different occasion for growth.

If you are staying on a step instead of taking a step upwards, don't think of it as being stuck, especially if you are constantly learning. I see staying on a step as providing yourself consistency. Consistency allows you to repeat habits, keep boundaries in place, and speak kind words to yourself. Staying on a step to find repeatable patterns that are working for you is just as important as changing or adding something new.

Going back to those high-achieving perfectionist tendencies, the reason we strive for perfection is to have control. Well, guess what? You now have control through consistency that offers certainty, which deactivates your FF response. It is in moments like this when you can give your inner cheerleader the opportunity to improve your mood and ease stress. Choosing to take care of yourself is your inner cheerleader congratulating you on a job well done. Own that, woman!

I've said this once, and I'll say it a thousand times over: self-care isn't glamorous. **When navigating stress, worry, anxiety, and burnout, it is the day-to-day routines, habits, and words you choose to use that are important.** It is not the elaborate vacations, random spa days, or someone writing a rave review about you. It is the dirty, hard work that comes from determining what your wants and needs are and then speaking to yourself kindly. For the high achiever, taking control of self-care makes you more resilient to step into times of uncertainty.

Now, I'm going to take you through two specific routines: morning and bedtime. The mornings are crucial because you get to set your intention for the day. At the end of the day, resetting and listening to that inner cheerleader gives you the opportunity to step into active rest, set intentions around sleep, and nourish your being.

My current morning routine is as follows:

1. The moment I wake up, which is usually before my alarm goes off, I listen to an audiobook, meditation app, or mindset course for about thirty minutes. I stay lying in bed, as I can't fall back asleep once I'm awake. I give myself the leniency to be over or under the thirty minutes; it usually isn't exactly thirty minutes.
2. I breathe, create intentions for the day and work through any thoughts that may be blocking me to pump myself up. (Literally! I fist-pump the air sometimes!) First thing in the morning is when my mind runs a mile a minute; I kid you not, it moves so fast that if I don't harness it, I'm exhausted by mid-morning.

   If you ever notice that you wake up in a panic or start

stressing the moment your alarm goes off, that's a normal physiological response based on the chemicals circulating your body. Through the night, the level of cortisol (your stress hormone) rises and is high in the morning. If your cortisol is high, and your body has already armed you for the day, then you get to figure out how to harness that energy for the good.

3. After I have finished harnessing my mind, I get out of bed, get dressed, brush my teeth, and sit on the floor with my puppy. I lay my yoga mat on the floor. I turn on a playlist I chose the night before (this conserves that ME in my tank). Then I dance, stretch, and move my body. Whatever movement comes up, I allow to happen. If that means I'm doing fifty squats, flowing through downward dog, or moving to the beat of the music, great! The key is to create movement in your body to release some of the cortisol that was built up. Movement helps calm the mind and also improves muscle strength and joint mobility for later in life.
4. Once the next alarm goes off (yes, I set two alarms; the second is to let me know it's time to move out of mindset and bodyset routines), I put on make-up, deodorant, and my signature perfume, then head to the kitchen to brew myself a hot beverage. I rarely drink coffee or tea, and when I do, it is decaffeinated. Removing caffeine from my diet has decreased my anxiety and leveled my mood . . . as a bonus, it has also helped improve my sleep. As the water boils, I take my vitamins.

This routine never lets me down. Does it evolve from time to time? Totally. However, I know that whenever the routine starts to slip, it means something in my life has shifted and it's time to reflect. Being a high achiever, I find it easy to get up in the morning and immediately run to my computer and start work. Old

Jessica sacrificed herself based on her previous definitions of success and happiness (or what she thought they were). It required rewriting and hardwiring a new hiking trail to let myself know I am more important than any work I am trying to accomplish.

The one thing I absolutely will no longer do before my morning routine is check social media or review emails, texts, or messages. Those things will amplify my already racing mind, causing me to slip into anxiousness, worry, overthinking, and feeling like I'm already behind, affecting how the rest of my day unfolds. Because I know that, I create an intention around my day, check in with myself, and pump myself up before I head into a day filled with uncertainty.

You are likely wondering what time I get up in the morning. I will not share that, because the whole point of describing my morning self-care regimen is not for you to replicate it exactly, but for you to figure out your own personalized routine. Whether you get up at four-thirty or ten o'clock, starting off the day in a way where you feel in control and speak kindly to yourself is the most important thing. Remember, it's important for you to do you!

Let's now move toward your evening and bedtime routine. This is equally as important as your morning because it sets you up to slow your body down and ease your mind. I don't think it gets talked about enough. If your bedtime routine is overshadowed and you wake up depleted, you can't step into a morning with a full ME tank.

You've likely heard of some bedtime tips already: no blue light, shut off your phone one hour before bed, get electronics out of your bedroom, and keep the temperature cool. These are great, but your evening and bedtime routine should reflect what you need and want to soothe, replenish, and calm you down.

Here are some suggestions to include in your evening routine, and don't worry, you don't have to incorporate all of them. Pick and choose one or two that work for you:

- Putting a time limit on your venting session about work or something that pissed you off
- Making or buying a healthy dinner (including dessert if you want it)
- Chatting with a loved one
- Moving your body through some sort of exercise (yes, it can be a walk or stretching)
- Going to bed at a similar time each night (and scheduling this into your calendar)
- Organizing your thoughts for the next day
- Engaging in intimacy (with yourself or a partner—heck, this can be any time of the day)
- Accepting emotions you experienced during the day

Accepting emotions can be tough at times because your mind constantly thinks, but you don't have to process every little thing before you go to sleep. Accepting your feelings and recognizing you will tackle them tomorrow helps settle the mind. Matthew Walker, author of *Why We Sleep*, talks about the saying "sleep on it" and why in the morning we often wake up with solutions to problems we thought about the night before. Our brain, that problem-solving machine, still works during the different subconscious stages of sleep. This is why, after a good night's sleep, you wake up without brain fog, able to navigate the challenges of the day.

The actual sleep part is important—this should be top priority and a non-negotiable. Now don't get me wrong, there will still be some nights I let myself sacrifice sleep to hang out with a friend. Do I feel shitty the next morning? No, because hanging out with my friend also replenished my energy. You have to navigate what works for you. The number of years that sleep was an afterthought caught up with me when I wasn't regulating my inner critic. I relied on multiple cups of caffeine, and my emotions controlled every aspect of my day. There were days I felt physically ill because I didn't get enough sleep. I even thought that living in brain fog was normal. Never in a million years did I think sleep was productive. Society and company culture glamorize overworking until you are exhausted; but what was I actually gaining? A whole lot of unhappiness and a whole lot of heartburn.

Nowadays I have an alarm clock for bed. It's not like I immediately walk over to my bed, shut off my mind, and go straight to sleep when the alarm goes off. It signals my mind that it's time to slowly start to wind down. It's me telling myself: *Stop whatever you are doing, turn on the dishwasher, let the dog out, head to the bathroom to brush your teeth, put your phone on do not disturb, set your alarm, and hop into bed to read your current romance novel.*

And yes, when I first started this routine, I had to actively communicate with myself because my inner critic would try to convince me that another episode of TV or working just a bit longer would be all I needed to feel better. My mind and body have a limit; the same is true for all of us. When we start to pay attention to our limits, we can listen to them more. For example, you want to have a few chocolate chip cookies? Great, take four and let yourself know that any more than that and you'll feel gross. Don't take the sleeve of cookies, convincing yourself you deserve it and then feel like shit afterwards. Same holds true for alcohol, social media, shopping, etc. Finding and setting your limits and expectations while building your inner cheerleader up will take time to figure out.

It took me almost three years to notice that I can't read nonfiction books before bed, as I would slip into note-taking mode instead of settling into slumber. Another definitive boundary I put in place is that any conversations with my mother must be concluded at least three hours before I go to bed. My relationship with my mother is still challenging, and I tend to get wound up after speaking to her.

Every now and then, even to this day, I take a sleeping pill. Something we haven't yet talked about are medications. So, "I'd like to take a minute, just sit right there, I'll tell you how I" gave myself permission to take an anti-anxiety and anti-depression medication. (If you missed the reference, I was quoting the theme song from *The Fresh Prince of Bel Air*). For the longest time I fought taking medications because I thought it meant I was admitting defeat to mental illness. The same psychiatrist who told me I was experiencing burnout shared words of wisdom that I now will share with you. To paraphrase: "If you decide to take these medications now, it doesn't mean you will be on them for the rest of your life. If they work, great; you have the capacity then to practice more brain training and figure out what works without feeling like you're up against a brick wall. If they don't work, then you try something else."

It was at this moment in time that I recognized the words I choose to use have value. How my psychiatrist chose to speak to me is how I wanted to speak to others, including my patients and clients. Words have value. Words have meaning. Changing and altering your words can help you see a different perspective, and perspective is what allows you to grow and learn. I left my psychiatrist's office that day with a glimmer of hope that everything I had worked toward was in fact worth it . . . that I was worth it.

Burnout, numbing behaviours, boundaries, active rest, creating healthy habits, and routines all play a part in how you choose to speak to yourself. Do you see how each of these builds upon the other? Do you see how all the cycles come together and how it all leads back to the voice you hear? If your inner critic is the loudest, then it is easy to head down the path of burnout. Numbing behaviours feel like they're helping when in reality they only dig you deeper into an abyss that is hard to escape. Your inner critic may not like the boundaries you implement, but your inner cheerleader will thank you when you give yourself permission to value your time, energy, and mental space. As you move through your healing process and allow your inner cheerleader to speak up, creating those healthy habits becomes more and more natural. You get to step into your confidence and worth—because, babe, you are more than enough; you only have to believe it. Gone are the days of sacrificing yourself only to make it to retirement. Give yourself the compassion to evolve as a human being and as a powerful, strong woman. If something isn't working for you, let your inner cheerleader step up and make the change.

PART IV

DARKNESS

"'There are different kinds of darkness,' Rhys said.
I kept my eyes shut.
'There is the darkness that frightens, the darkness that soothes, the darkness that is restful.'
I pictured each.
'There is the darkness of lovers, and the darkness of assassins. It becomes what the bearer wishes it to be, needs it to be. It is not wholly bad or good.'"
—*Sarah J. Maas, A Court of Mist and Fury*

CHAPTER 14

WHAT IS DARKNESS?

I will never forget my cell phone at home again, but on that winter day in 2007, I was already in class when I realized it wasn't in my backpack. *Whatever,* I thought, *I'll make it through the day and get it when I get home. It's not like anyone would need to get a hold of me.* This was my second year at university, and Facebook was in its second year, too. You had your computer, the internet, Facebook, and MSN. You didn't really need your cell phone because apps weren't a thing yet.

When I got back to my dorm that day in the late afternoon, my phone had twenty-three missed calls from my dad. There were no voicemails, only missed calls and text messages saying, "Call me." My initial reaction: something is most definitely wrong and I don't know what it could be. My thoughts started to race, and it felt like my heart was going to jump out of my chest. When I sat down and called my dad, it felt like time stopped; each ring when he didn't pick up felt like torture. When he answered, he told me my mom had been in a bad car accident and that the car was totalled but my mom was fine and at the hospital under observation. He instructed me to stay at school as the winter semester had recently started. I felt scared and helpless because I usually stepped into the caregiver role. Being away at university gave me a bit of solace, but I constantly felt guilt that I should be doing more.

Facetime didn't exist, and Skype wasn't really a thing, so I called my mom the same day through the hospital inpatient phone line because I was also in such a panic. I needed to know if she was okay and needed to hear it from her. I remember sitting at my desk, listening to my mom's voice. Her voice was disjointed and raspy but she said she was fine. I was relieved although something still gnawed at me in the pit of my stomach. Because I usually catastrophized, relief was never fully embraced as I waited for the "other shoe to drop." She proceeded to tell me about her injuries and that she had bumps and bruises, a torn eyelid, and a shredded ligament in her knee but everything else seemed fine, or so I thought.

It wasn't until I was emailed photos of the car months later that I realized how brutal the accident had been. My family chose to keep vital information from me because they said school should be my focus. I later found out the doctors diagnosed her with experiencing a cardiac syncope event, which is a temporary loss of consciousness due to insufficient blood to the brain. It's a medical term for having fainted or passed out.

In this situation, it happened to my mom while she was driving on a sunny afternoon to pick up my brother from high school. At the time, the school was in an undeveloped town, out in the country. Roads in and out of the school were only two lanes, one going each direction. From what the bus driver described to the police in the full report, my mom started to drift into his lane, crossing the midline toward his oncoming school bus full of kids. Thankfully, he reacted quickly and angled the bus so my mom's car tucked right under the middle, reducing the amount of impact and injuries. The bus driver and kids sustained no physical injuries.

Unfortunately, the car took most of the impact. The car had no airbag because it was thirteen years old. My mom's body, having gone limp due to the lack of consciousness, collapsed the steering wheel. When the paramedics and firefighters arrived on scene, they had to use the "jaws of life" rescue tool (Google it if you don't know what it is) to get my mom out of the car. She was rushed to the emergency department.

Due to the nature of the accident and the car having to be opened like a can opener to get my mom out, the car was impounded. When my dad arrived to remove the car's contents, the clerk at the impound lot asked, "Did she survive?" When I tell you I was given misleading information about the severity of the accident, I'm not kidding. It even made the town's headlines. The newspaper photos were emailed to me, and when I saw them, I was speechless. The car was unrecognizable. It looked like a scrap of metal with the bus in the background.

My mother, coherent with me on the phone a day later, was in a wheelchair for a few months due to the torn knee ligament. She went through rehab, and to this day she wears a knee brace and uses a cane from time to time. Her eyelid tear healed but she still has a slight scar. All in all, she appeared to be physically doing as well as could be. Yet, one thing would never heal: her traumatic brain injury (TBI).

This was my mom's third TBI. As she was already bipolar, this brain injury amplified existing symptoms and triggered new ones, including psychosis. The psychosis ranged from thinking the FBI was out to get her to thinking I was my evil twin when I came to visit. I had to show her my driver's license at times to reassure her I was who I said I was. That was rough.

Eventually, she moved into my maternal grandparents' house, because my dad and brother needed help taking care of her. It was during this time that my mother's side of the family began to fully understand my mom's mental illness. Mental health wasn't really talked about even though we as a family experienced it firsthand. Navigating mental health concerns was and still is an experience unique to each generation based on societal and cultural norms. This is why it is still hard to talk about anxiety, depression, burnout, perfectionism, and impostor phenomenon because there are still stigmas associated with them.

Just the other day, on a Facebook group that I am in, someone wrote, "My theory is that when you hear mental health mental health mental health 24/7, you start questioning your own sanity." There will always be people who don't believe in or disagree with mental health conversations because they aren't physical illnesses. No one questions why my mom walks with a cane, but her bipolar symptoms are much harder for people to understand. Similarly, some people find it hard to accept that high achievers experience mental health issues. When I, a person with no visible physical ailments, received mental health diagnoses, I wanted to blend in as much as possible, but I struggled internally. When I started telling the people closest to me what was going on, they were in disbelief. I hid it for so long because I didn't want to be viewed as someone who wasn't strong enough or couldn't get her shit together. I didn't want others to pity me nor did I want it to come across as if I was using it as an excuse. I know I'm not the only one who has felt something similar.

If someone you know has cancer and is undergoing treatment, you may notice the person develops hair loss, grey skin, and significant weight loss. The person going through cancer may undergo months of therapy and years of healing. You would never tell that cancer patient to "suck it up" or say they are using it as an excuse, would you? Then why is it okay to say to someone struggling with their inner voice or mental health to "suck it up"? Telling someone to "suck it up" discounts their experience and emotions.

Let's take a hot minute to talk about the difference between *toxic positivity* and *informed optimism.* I know some people will tell you, "Just put a smile on, it will get better," or "You should be happy and thankful for all you have." My response: this is toxic positivity to the core. Forcing sunshine onto someone who doesn't feel it won't make them feel more positive than usual. In fact, you're undermining them by discounting how they feel.

Here's another tidbit—you can't feel thankful for something if you are deep down in the dumps. Yes, gratitude practice helps with anxiety, but if you're experiencing compassion fatigue (as we talked about in Part III, Burnout), it's hard to be grateful if you're putting out fires, spreading yourself too thin, constantly helping others, and living in your own darkness.

Informed optimism recognizes you can sit in your darkness and that it will pass. I love nature analogies so here goes another one: Toxic positivity is looking up at the sky when it's raining and having someone tell you, "No, it's sunny, too. You must believe it's sunny. You must find the sun." But you actually see rain and clouds. You feel the gusting wind and rain and maybe even hail on your face. Informed optimism recognizes it's raining and that when it's over, the sun will come out again. It's knowing that the hurt, darkness, sadness, and anger you feel will pass, just like a storm. The difference between the two is perspective and the words you use. If you want to believe in your positivity, use words that have better meaning.

Even when we struggle, we don't need to get angry at ourselves. We can use a kinder voice to acknowledge that we're struggling and remind ourselves that it's okay, the struggle won't be there forever. It is not the thought that distresses us, but the thought about our thoughts that causes the most suffering. If we can change the perspective of the thought, then we can adjust how we feel about it and how that shows up in our bodyset.

Don't get me wrong, it's challenging. Though I've navigated through my past life experiences, sometimes they come back and bite me in the ass. I mentioned this before in Part III. It's as if a thought of a thought triggers and resurfaces so I am reminded of how far I have come, but that I still have more work to do. Instead of beating myself up and thinking, *Well shit, why are you crying about this again, you've already worked through this,* my perspective changes and I ask, *What are you still looking to learn?* or *What didn't you learn the last time?*

It is in these moments that I recognize being human comes with ups and downs, trials and tribulations, peaks and valleys, and all the analogies you can think of. Not every day can be sunshine, rainbows, and unicorns but it doesn't have to feel like you are being consumed by your darkness, where your inner critic keeps a hold of you.

If we reflect back to Part I, I shared you should start a positive investment container for that rainy day. This is where it comes in handy because on those rainy days—or let's be real, the crap-tastic days—you can pull from the container. If *positive investment container* doesn't fit into your vocabulary, call it show-and-tell, a piggy bank, or whatever you want. In the finance world, we have RRSP, Roth IRAs, stocks, and cryptocurrency. All of these are forms of long-term investment, which is what you are building with your positive investment container. It is your inner cheerleader who chooses to invest. If you don't invest, then you don't get to draw on it when a rainy day happens, and you don't get to lean on your inner cheerleader. If you actively invest, then you can show yourself the evidence you have been building up over time—evidence that you are capable, successful and worthy—and it's evidence you can believe because it's in plain sight.

BRAIN TRAINING EXERCISE: POSITIVE INVESTMENT CONTAINER, CONSISTENCY EDITION

If you haven't started your container yet or you haven't added to it in some time, take a moment right here and now to do so. Reflect on you being you, then write a kind note to yourself and put it in your container.

CHAPTER 15

TRUST SQUAD

I remember the exact moment I found out. It was one o'clock in the morning and I had just returned home from a night shift as a desk clerk at one of the university dormitories. It was now a few months after my mom's car accident. My roommate at the time, Tyler, had texted me during my shift and told me to wake him up when I got home. I didn't understand, but it sounded as if he had something interesting to share. So, I went with it. I walked into his bedroom and gently woke him up.

He sat up in the bed and said, "You have to call your dad."

I huffed, "What? No way. I'll call him in the morning."

Tyler replied, "No, call him now and I'm going to sit right here."

I still didn't understand and started to feel a little panicked. There was no way I could have predicted what came next.

I rang my dad, "What's up?"

He sounded tired. "Are you sitting and are you with Tyler?"

I hesitated and responded slowly, "*Yaah?*" I paused and drew out the words, "What's. . . up?"

This was the norm in my family; there was always something going on. So, I braced myself. I can't remember exactly what I braced myself for: likely something to do with my mom, since she just had that car accident, or the death of a grandparent or even the death of our family dog, Ginger. Yet, none of those words were spoken that night.

Instead, his voice crackled as he said, "Daniela is gone."

Daniela was my fifteen-year-old cousin—not by blood, but, in Italian culture, my cousin. We grew up together. Her grandparents were my mother's godparents, my parents were Daniela's godparents, and I was her sponsor for confirmation. Having been raised Catholic, I felt honored to be chosen; church was a large part of our culture. Only five years older than Daniela, I felt like her big sister.

"Where did she go?"

"Daniela is no longer with us."

I was still confused and started to worry. "Okay . . . so did you call the cops? . . . Who is out looking for her?"

He proceeded to tell me that Daniela died and that she had taken her own life. I can't really remember time passing after that. All I know is that I went into do-what-needs-to-be-done mode, which is when I lose all sense of time and feeling. This is more than just my usual FF response. I coordinated train tickets home, confirmed times with my father, asked about the other family members, picked my black outfits, wondered if my mom's medication was up-to-date, and if we needed to call the psychiatrist to adjust medication, and asked how my brother was doing. At the end of the conversation, my dad asked to speak with Tyler and I passed the phone over.

The next thing I remember was lying down on the bed in my work outfit while Tyler lay next to me. He didn't want me to be alone. There were no tears. I got up the next morning about an hour or two later to catch the train back to the city. The next days were a blur, but I do remember sitting in the pew behind Daniela's mom as she screeched and wailed and howled. I will never forget that sound. Still, I shed no tears.

I checked in on my cousin, Daniela's brother, to make sure he was doing okay. Then the next thing I knew, I was back at school studying. I drowned myself in school, work, partying, and making out with guys. No, Tyler and I weren't a couple. Tyler was someone I would call a member of my trust squad. Today, he is no longer in that trust squad—we lost touch after graduation—but during that time in my life, when I didn't even know what a trust squad was, Tyler was in it.

A trust squad includes people you go to when you aren't feeling yourself and you are in that deep, dark abyss. These are also the people with whom you share awesome things that are happening in your life. These members will be excited for your successes and cheer you on. You can truly and genuinely trust these individuals. When you trust someone wholly, you can share the uncomfortable and sensitive topics without the fear of being judged, criticized, or ridiculed. You can also share the amazingness that happens, and these individuals will support your endeavours and achievements. You know these people aren't your competition, but rather your cheerleaders.

That August, a few months after Daniela died, one of my friends saw that I was struggling. Laura and I had been hanging out all summer, and it was a blast; but she knew my emotions were like a storm cloud. To most people I came across as happy, pulled-together, and moving along in life, but Laura could see right through it.

We were driving to her house when she blatantly said to me, "We're going to talk about this. We're going to talk about what happened."

As I sat in the passenger seat next to her, I whipped my head toward her. "I'm *fine*."

"I know you're fine, but we're still going to chat about it."

We were on the way back to Laura's house to make dinner and hang out. I felt like a toy boat circling the bathtub drain. Everything from that moment on moved in slow motion: getting out of the car, opening the house door, making and eating dinner, and finally sitting down. Laura looked at me with kind eyes, and the dam burst. Every emotion I had been holding deep down for months flowed out in a seismic wave.

I blamed myself because I was away at university and didn't have time for Daniela. I was frustrated because I didn't understand why it happened. I was hateful and infuriated with the bullies who picked on her. Most of all, I was so unbelievably sad, empty, and powerless because the future I envisioned for her abruptly ended.

My head dropped to my hands, tears flowed like a river, and it hurt to breathe. In that instant, the crushing embrace that Laura provided me was the support I never knew I needed; *this* is a trust squad member. Today, Laura and I only drop a text every couple of years, as our lives have grown apart. Nevertheless, Laura was instrumental in putting back a piece of my heart that had a massive hole in it. She gave me the space to share my dark inner voice when it had been silently screaming at me.

Trust evolves over time. Trust may be pushed to its limits, and it is up to you to decide whether or not you want to navigate those relationships. With Tyler and Laura, a natural progression happened where we left university and went our separate ways. It's important to constantly evaluate your trust squad members to accurately decide if they are people you can, in fact, lean on. There have been many times I have put the wrong people into my trust squad, including family, friends, and coworkers.

Over time I found it easier to isolate rather than open up to people. After speaking with Laura, I rebuilt that dam and stopped sharing. It hurt too much. Plus, as I wrote back in Part I, I had been told at an early age that I shouldn't be sharing my emotions, and because I wanted to be a dentist, I thought I had to be tough and strong. I shoved everything back into that anxiety box and kept going. But loneliness is not just a feeling but a health threat as well.[44] Loneliness increases your odds of dying by 45 percent while excessive drinking and obesity increase your odds of dying by 30 percent and 20 percent, respectively.[45]

What I didn't realize was that Laura became my inner cheerleader that day. She gave me a glimpse of what my inner voice was capable of becoming. Over the years, both my inner voice and the voices of my friends have played significant roles in my becoming who I am today. It is important to develop meaningful relationships where you feel like you belong and can trust someone entirely. When choosing trust squad members, there is a saying I like to live by: "People come into your life for a reason, a season, or a lifetime. You become hurt when you place them in the wrong group." Let's just sit with that for a minute. Both Tyler and Laura came into my life for a reason and a few seasons.

Currently, my trust squad has only a handful of members, but I wouldn't have it any other way. These are the people who can help me question my inner critic and be my inner cheerleader when I don't have the strength to be my own. Just as important as speaking kindly to yourself is choosing people who will speak kindly to you. You do not need to do it alone.

BRAIN TRAINING EXERCISE: TRUST SQUAD MEMBERS

Who is in your trust squad? You likely have a few individuals who come to mind. These are the people you can genuinely trust and be vulnerable with. Then there may be other people you aren't so sure about. Here are a few yes/no questions you can ask yourself when deciding who belongs in your trust squad:

1. Is this person consistent?
2. Is this person compassionate?

3. Does this person respect your boundaries?
4. Does this person share other people's information? If so, does that worry you that they will share your information?
5. Does your person confide in you?
6. Is your person open-minded?
7. Does this person make time for you?
8. Does the person actively listen?
9. Do you make time for this person so they know they are important to you?

I have an exercise worksheet to assist you with these questions. Head over to the book portal, www.speakkindlyyourelistening.com, to get access.

CHAPTER 16

WHY SHOULD YOU CHANGE YOUR INNER CRITIC?

Up until now, we've talked about Impostor Phenomenon (IP), Perfectionism, and Burnout as separate and linked entities. However, I haven't yet shared with you *why* it is important to change your inner voice. Here are the three reasons why:

1. FEAR OF FAILURE VS. BELIEF FOR SUCCESS

There is a massive difference in how you choose to show up if you think you are going to fail versus if you think you are going to succeed. Let's say you are about to pitch an idea to a client, boss, colleague, or friend. If you automatically think they are going to think your idea is stupid and crap, then no matter how the pitch goes, you will likely see it as a failure. If it goes poorly, the way you spoke to yourself is evidence your idea was crap to begin with, so you'll think future ideas are crap, too, and it will prevent you from pitching again. If your idea went well, maybe it will come with a short confidence boost, but then it's easy to ruminate and pick it apart until you've picked yourself apart. Good or bad, the pitch failed.

But if you open yourself up for curiosity, interest, and compassion, then you will believe you are capable. If you change from the fear of failure to the belief of success, then you can change the way you speak to yourself, change how you show up, and change how you deliver the pitch. Now, if the pitch goes poorly, you can look back and be curious about what you can do differently next time instead of picking yourself apart. If the pitch goes well, then you look back and step into your confidence. The difference in your words changes the inner critic to the inner cheerleader.

This holds true for any adventure in life, not just a pitch. If you choose to reframe and believe in the potential for success, the potential for a desired outcome, and the potential for informed optimism, then regardless of the aftermath, your inner cheerleader can navigate through. There is a table later in this chapter that gives you examples on how to change your inner critic to an inner cheerleader.

2. THE MINDSET–BODYSET CONNECTION

We've talked about this already but I'm going to sum it up right here: Your mind speaks to your body, and your body speaks to your mind. It is a constant feedback loop. If you tell yourself you can't do something and that creates discomfort by activating your FF response, then that FF response will feed the information to your mind, confirming you can't do something. In order to get out of the loop, you can change your words from inner critic to inner cheerleader. This reminds your FF response that you are safe and capable. Once your FF response knows that, you can break the loop instead of getting stuck in it year after year after year.

All my clients previously mentioned in this book have said their FF response doesn't feel as intense after working through their mindset–bodyset connection. Do they all still experience an FF response? Well, yeah. That's all a part of being human. But now, they understand their mindset–bodyset connection. I've heard too many stories of women finally applying for a promotion, getting it, then IP kicking into full gear that makes them think they don't want it anymore. It's not that these women actually don't want it anymore, it's because of how scared, fearful, and uncomfortable it makes them. Let me ask you this: don't you want to step into your potential without the fear that you're never enough? It's totally possibly to manage your inner critic so you can create a new and improved feedback loop. If you are looking for an in-depth review of the mindset–bodyset connection, check out the book *The Body Keeps Score* by Dr. Bessel Van Der Kolk.

3. THE "CRASH" AFTER THE GO-GO-GO

For the high achiever, society has defined productivity as go-go-go. You have to be moving and doing or setting another goal and climbing that next mountain. That go-go-go comes with consequences such as mental, physical, and spiritual illness. You don't need to be mentally or emotionally broken to take a break. You do not need to hustle or overextend yourself to then give yourself the permission to rest, play, or have fun. If you reflect on the times you were exhausted or became ill, how many of those were associated with overworking or spreading yourself too thin? I can tell you the exact times I have become sick because they always landed on weekends, breaks, vacations, or staycations. During those times, just like when I drank myself into oblivion, I turned into a blob. That crash comes with depleted energy and a dark abyss that I had a hard time getting out of. However, becoming a blob meant I didn't feel guilty for resting, though it didn't feel good because I was sick. That meant I didn't get to enjoy the break or nurture myself with rest, play, or fun.

When I realized how important it was to change the way I spoke to myself, which was when I was in my deepest, darkest despair, I knew it meant putting in the hard work. I knew there would be days of joy and days of sorrow, but I couldn't allow my inner critic to run my mind. That voice is the darkness that frightens me.

CHAPTER 17

CHANGING YOUR INNER CRITIC

For years, I thought I was broken. From the age of fourteen, I knew I wanted to be a dentist. Every decision I made went into becoming a dentist. I worked so hard and beat myself up, comparing myself to other students who did more or did better than me. In the fourth grade, when we learned haikus and everyone rhymed their names, I came up with "Jess is a mess." That stuck to me like gum sticks to long hair: tangled, woven, and hard to remove.

It wasn't until I was twenty when I was diagnosed with a learning disability in reading comprehension. You think it would have eased how I thought of myself. Instead, it only made it worse. That diagnosis led to self-doubt and calling myself stupid, incapable, and a loser. I carried those hateful words about myself for years, and it contributed to how I saw my own worth as a high achiever, as a human and as a woman. Time and time again, that inner critic fed me false information: *You're not smart, you're not meant to achieve those dreams, you look ugly, you're not as skinny as other girls, you aren't good at sports, sooooo you're not really good at anything. What's wrong with you?* The lies and comparisons I kept feeding myself were all a part of the story behind my inner critic. Unfortunately for many of us, that story gets written in those early years as a child, teenager, and young adult, and then we carry those words forward into our adulthood. In the next few chapters, this is where you will learn precisely how to change your inner critic.

For me, I always felt like I needed to prove myself to family, friends, and society. There was that high-achieving mentality where if I got good grades, then there was a chance I could walk around with my head held high. That's also what the schooling system does: praise children for getting high grades and fitting in. Because of the challenges at home, school was the one thing I had absolute control over. If I worked hard, then it showed. However, my inner critic used the environment around me to say mean and ugly things, beating me up along the way. As I write this, I can still stare into the eyes of my seventeen-year-old inner critic. It is a monster in the night, creeping along the darkness, telling me, *You don't look like those girls in the magazines. You're a big, fat loser, and nobody likes you. You don't have any real friends or family.* All I desperately wanted was to belong.

Let's revisit that moment in math class I talked about in Part I, when Brent saw my grade in math class and commented, "You're actually *smart?*" My inner critic that day stole Brent's words and hardwired them into my brain. I said this to myself over and over again. Single moments or comments can still haunt us decades later. My inner critic would use these words and rewrite a new, mean, and rude script each year, belittling me until my inner cheerleader was the size of an ant. The only inner voice I heard was my inner critic: *You're never going to get into dental school. You're going to be a loser because you can't amount to anything. Everyone thinks you're not smart. You're never going to make enough money.* When I finally got into dental school, I had convinced myself that my inner critic was the best motivator ever. Period. I knew no different. Somewhere deep in my mind, my inner critic had convinced me that my sole survival technique was to belittle and depreciate myself. Eventually, that's all I believed: that I would never be enough for anyone or anything.

Year after year, any time my inner cheerleader tried to make an appearance, my inner critic tricked her into standing over a trap door. Each time, my inner critic pulled the lever and the trap door swallowed my inner cheerleader whole. Smirking, my inner critic continued to use those unkind words and placed me in a darkness where my heart hurt and my mind was seeded with hurtful phrases. I know the saying goes, "Sticks and stones may break your bones but words will never hurt," but that's an absolute lie. I've said it earlier and will say it again: every word you choose to say to yourself has purpose, meaning, and power. Every single word plays a role in how you view yourself, your identity and your worth. If your inner critic is the only one you hear, then your confidence experiences death by a thousand cuts.

The worst was when my inner critic would say, *They are only saying that because they're your friend. They have to say that. It's not what they actually believe.* When these words were spoken, the only voice heard was my inner critic, nothing else. There was no internal dialogue between my inner critic and cheerleader because my cheerleader was so afraid of my inner critic.

Even while my mom recovered, she pushed me to connect with the university and share my diagnosis. If it wasn't for her, I wouldn't have received extra time on exams nor the help to navigate a different learning style. A part of my learning disability is that I couldn't see the big picture or how all the small intricate details formed the bigger picture. I got bogged down in the details and could memorize everything in a textbook but couldn't figure out how they all came together. At first, I thought of my learning disability as a massive disruption and hindrance to my life. Now, I see it for the opportunity it turned into. I got to learn how to learn all over again, to understand there are different teaching and learning styles, and to become the educator I am today. Whatever title you want to give me—instructor, teacher, lecturer, speaker, educator, or coach—my goal is to share information in unique ways so you can think differently and change your narrative.

Today, because of that learning disability, I honed my skills in creative and critical thinking, problem-solving, communicating, decision-making, organization, and time management. I no longer consider myself as having a learning disability because I figured out my strengths and changed how I chose to speak to myself. By changing how I spoke to myself, it changed how I perceived me.

My weaknesses became my greatest assets when I actively sought the things I was good at and then commended myself for those skills. One of the reasons I had a hard time hearing my inner cheerleader was because of how society viewed my skills. They are considered "soft" skills, and calling them "soft" made me feel weak. For a very long time, my inner critic used that against me by saying those skills weren't important, weren't enough, which I then interpreted as *I am not enough.*

To this day, society still holds technical skills in higher regard, but I can see a shift happening, especially with individuals like Brené Brown, Adam Grant, and Simon Sinek having more conversations around these topics. Workplace cultures are noticing higher employee turnover due to employees feeling under-appreciated. Leaders today need to think creatively, communicate effectively, and problem-solve from multiple perspectives. Therefore, "soft" skills should now be called *essential* skills, just as I wrote previously in Part I. If your inner critic has been saying, "Well, critical thinking is a 'soft' skill and you still have to prove yourself," I want you to change those words to, "Critical thinking is an essential skill that I am quite good at." Change your words and notice how your inner cheerleader will start doing backflips in joy. This is how you start to change your inner voice: changing the words you use and finding the evidence to go with those words. It's hard work, but it's totally worth it.

It is really easy in today's overworking culture to think you aren't good enough because you don't have certain letters, degrees, or certificates behind your name. I don't want you to think this is holding you back from being your confident self. No number of certificates will help you step into that confidence if you don't start changing how you choose to speak to yourself and believing in your abilities. Let's start here and now.

1. EXAMINE YOUR INNER VOICE

First and foremost, you have to pay attention to how you speak to yourself and examine the words you actively say. This is similar to creating self-awareness, which we chatted about in Part I. Take in the when, why, where, and with whom. There is no need to change what you are saying yet. All you have to do is notice it. During this time, it can be really easy for you to get angry at yourself because you are wondering, "Why can't I catch myself before I say it?" or, "I can't believe I'm saying that again." Regardless, you are navigating new territory, and as you do, think of this stage as information gathering. You can't make changes if you don't first know what the inner critic is saying to keep you stuck.

2. ALTER YOUR THOUGHT

Once you have noticed what you are saying, it's time to start changing your thought from *self-doubt* to *idea doubt. Idea doubt* is when you can separate yourself from the task and the blame. For example, let's say you had a conversation with a client and it didn't go as planned. Instead of walking away saying, "I suck at explaining new ideas" (self-doubt), you can change it to, "The idea wasn't fully delivered as expected" (idea doubt). That way you can reflect and figure out what you can do different next time instead of ruminating about how you're not good enough. Idea doubt can be energizing, leading you to find solutions and get specific, while self-doubt can be debilitating. Adam Grant discusses this in one of his TED Talks, "The Surprising Habits of Original Thinkers."

3. SUBSTITUTE YOUR WORDS

This one I find fun and frustrating at the same time. There are three I'll talk about:

1. ***Expectation versus curiosity:*** As I've talked about earlier, there is a difference between saying, "Well, I hope today is a good day," versus "I'm curious how today will unfold." When you set a specific expectation around the day, anything that goes wrong and disrupts your day, you interpret as: "Today is a bust." By allowing curiosity to enter instead, then a day that doesn't go exactly as planned doesn't disappoint you as much.
2. ***Apologizing:*** You do not need to apologize for everything. When you apologize for something that was out of your control or when you didn't actually do something wrong, your inner critic takes that information and associates it with a negative emotion. For example, instead of saying "I'm sorry for running late," you can substitute "Thank you for your patience." This substitution will create a shift in dynamics within yourself and with the person you are talking to.
3. ***Clarifying word substitution from negative to positive:*** It can be quite easy to speak in a negative tone to protect or motivate yourself. However, speaking negatively to yourself time and time again means you think and feel in the negative only. This is likely the simplest change although the hardest one

to believe. It is going from words like *I can't* to *I can,* or *I'm not capable* to *I am capable.*

4. EVALUATE HOW YOU REACTED

Initially when you practice steps 1 through 3, you may get frustrated with yourself, thinking it isn't working. I can reassure you it is, and evaluating how your body reacts is one cue. I've talked about the FF response before and what it can feel like: butterflies in your stomach, a lump in your throat, or a faster heart rate. You're going to see if that FF response has settled a bit . . . if it feels different in your body. If you start to feel a sense of ease, then you know you believe what you say. You can do this by ranking it on a belief scale (zero being you don't believe your words at all, and ten being you wholeheartedly believe your words). If you changed *I can't* to *I can* and you rank a two on the scale, but the next time you bump up to two-and-a-half then you are slowly starting to believe it. Scales are helpful because they are subjective, just like a pain scale in the doctor's office. Don't compare your belief scale to anyone else's. You are the only one who needs to believe the words you choose to use.

When you practice steps one through four, I want to remind you the process takes time. It could be months or years until your inner cheerleader is the predominant voice. You may even work through something and then years later it gets triggered and you have to work through it again. Nothing is wrong with you. Something has come up that makes you realize there is more work to be done. It's easy for your inner critic to jump back in, but if you view it as another stage of practice or healing, then you don't need to feel like you're jammed back into that corner. It becomes easier to recognize and change what your inner critic says. Use each day as a learning opportunity to step into your truest potential by allowing your inner cheerleader to show you that you are worthy.

HOW TO REFRAME FROM INNER CRITIC TO INNER CHEERLEADER

Inner Critic Voice	Reframe to Inner Cheerleader Voice
"You're not meant to achieve these dreams. They're someone else's."	"If you know what you want, then you can go get it. Your dreams can be similar to someone else's too, but you know what yours are."
"Who do you think you are?"	"You feel out of place and discouraged, but you know you can do this. Because if not you, then who?"
"You don't have enough time."	"You can reset your expectations and define your priorities to fit your schedule."
"Who cares?"	"You care. That's what matters."
"No one wants to hear your story."	"You're brave and courageous to share your story."
"What is wrong with you?"	"You feel like you have done something wrong. Take a moment to feel and ask yourself a different question."
"You've been talking too much, and people have stopped listening."	"You know the message you want to get across, and it will find the people who are a right fit."

Inner Critic Voice	Reframe to Inner Cheerleader Voice
"You're going to mess up."	"You're going to try, and know you may not get it right the first time . . . or second time. But eventually, you'll get it."
"You're not fast enough."	"You're developing skills, and that takes time. You're working toward being at a speed that works for you."
"You suck."	"You're having difficulty right now but it won't be forever."
"You have to work yourself to death in order to feel seen or heard."	"You have finished X, Y, Z. You can take a break and it's okay to take a break. If you don't feel seen or heard, it may be time to reflect on 'why' instead of blaming yourself."
"You're alone and will always be alone."	"You can do things on your own. Sometimes you feel lonely, but you have people you love and trust."
"You aren't good enough."	"You are good," or "You are good at (fill in the blanks)," or "You are skilled at A, B, C." "You are capable of G, H, F." "You are focusing on A, B, C."

In the last example of the inner critic voice, what I believe to be one of the most important reframes is the removal of the word *enough.* Anytime my brain hears *enough,* I think there is a lack thereof and I could have done more. Some synonymous words to *enough* include *adequate, sufficient,* and *acceptable.* When I hear these words, I think I could have done more because who wants to be just adequate? But, other synonymous words to *enough* include *abundant, full,* and *complete,* yet, these usually aren't the first that come to mind. Let me remind you of the unhelpful thinking pattern we previously talked about in Part II, Perfectionism. Using the word *enough* should be its own unhelpful thinking pattern because of the value we put on this word. Using the word *enough,* even in a statement like, "I am more than enough," makes us think something is missing. So when you are reframing from inner critic to inner cheerleader, adjust words until you find ones that work for you.

CHAPTER 18

THE INNER GREMLIN

It was my twenty-ninth birthday and we planned on having the family over at my Nonna's house. This year had been difficult, as my twenty-four-year-old brother battled an alcohol addiction. The road to recovery has its ups and downs but at the time it felt like more downs than ups. Because of my birthday being in the middle of all these challenges, I didn't want to celebrate . . . but, my family insisted.

I'm not going to lie; I dislike celebrating my birthdays regardless (and it is something I still am working on today). I find it hard to be the "centre of attention" because it feels like there is even more pressure to make sure everyone around me has a good time and gets along. I know I put this pressure on myself, but up until that point, I had played the caregiver and mediator roles for so long that I had a hard time turning the pressure off.

It was getting close to dinner, and I was supposed to pick up my brother from an aunt's house. When I arrived, I chatted with my cousin in the hallway while I waited for my brother to emerge from another room. Fifteen minutes passed, and still my brother hadn't appeared. I didn't understand what was taking so long so I asked my cousin, "Where is he?"

My cousin replied, "In the washroom."

Now, my entire family is lactose intolerant so this is normal, but today I had a gut feeling something was wrong. I knocked on the bathroom door. "David, you okay?"

No response, but I could hear the sink water running.

Again, I knocked. "Hey David, just checking . . . everything okay?"

Again, no response.

I turned to my cousin. "What were you guys doing?"

"Jamming and recording music."

I knocked louder. "David, can you unlock the door for me?"

No response.

As I stood looking up at my six-foot-tall cousin, I said with utter sternness, "Did you smoke or drink anything?"

He shook his head no.

I knocked again and with a softer voice, said, "Hey Dave, can you help me by unlocking the door?"

I finally heard movement behind the door and then a click.

I turned the handle. There was my brother, also six feet tall, 210 pounds, hunched over the sink in a cloud of steam. He steadied himself with both hands, the sink water running. I looked into the mirror. The reflection of his eyes met mine and they were hollow. He was drunk. Without my cousin knowing, my brother had found alcohol and decided to drink. I walked into the bathroom and gently spoke, "Can you tell me what you drank?"

"Wine."

I took a deep breath and asked, "Only wine?"

"Vodka."

"How much did you drink?"

"I finished the bottle," he said, slurring his words.

"Which bottle did you finish, David?"

He swayed. "The vodka bottle."

"How much was in the bottle?"

"It was almost full."

"How big was the bottle?"

"A 2-6."

I finally understood how much my brother had drunk. He'd had not only some wine but almost an entire 700mL bottle of vodka. My brother was teetering on the brink of alcohol poisoning.

He kept repeating, "The steam makes me feel better."

I finally convinced him to come with me. As he stepped away from the sink and threw his arm over my shoulder, I explained we would drive slow over any bumps and would stop if needed. All the windows would be down so he could get some fresh air. I should have driven him straight to the hospital, but I didn't. It's taken some time to figure out why I didn't just drive him to the hospital that night, and I've realized I was afraid of what my family would say. This was the same year I was diagnosed with clinical depression, a generalized anxiety disorder, and burnout. I was so mentally destroyed that I was afraid any decision I made would be wrong and I would be blamed.

We slowly made our way down the hallway. I looked at my cousin while he stood there speechless. "It's okay, I have this from here."

I got my brother into the car and took him back to my Nonna's house. I helped him upstairs to his bedroom only minutes before the rest of my family arrived. I didn't want this birthday dinner anymore, and yet here I was getting ready to plaster on a smile to get through. Relations among family members were already strained; this would just be the icing on the cake. As everyone took their places, I sat at the head of the table. Everyone else besides me laughed and talked about their lives while I sat there with a forced smile, wondering how my brother was doing.

I heard movement upstairs so I excused myself from the table to go check on him. David had decided to leave his bedroom and head into the bathroom. I could hear the water running again, this time, the shower. The door was locked and I couldn't get in. I headed back downstairs, and both my mom and Nonna looked at me and said, "It's okay, he'll sleep it off and he'll be fine."

As I returned to my seat, everyone sat enjoying their meal while I listened for any movement upstairs. I was concerned he might fall and hit his head, lie down and choke on his own vomit, or potentially drown. He should have gone to the hospital for monitoring instead of me carefully listening for any distressed sounds. No one asked me to, but this is who I had become. This is who I thought I ought to be. This was the role I thrust myself into. My brother took a couple days to recover and to this day still navigates his own challenges.

I was angry and frustrated at the world around me. I was tired, oh so tired, of being a caregiver. I was tired of trying to be the perfect dentist and professional and superwoman. I was too tired to take care of me. As I sat at that dinner table, I didn't want to be alive anymore. I didn't want to feel unpretty, unhealthy, and imperfect. I didn't want to be not enough. This is where my inner critic had taken me. Here's the thing: suicide was never an option because I had too much responsibility in my life. I had also seen what my cousin's death had done to the family, so even though I had thoughts of what life would look like without me being around, there was never a time I tried.

This was one of my darkest moments in life; a darkness full of pain, sadness, and anger, when I just didn't want to feel anymore. It was not long after this moment that the same psychiatrist helped me through this darkness. He still doesn't know I had thoughts of not being alive, because I felt ashamed to share it with him. I was the doctor and caregiver helping others; I felt I shouldn't have anything wrong with me. In this darkness, my inner critic defined me as useless, stupid, and meaningless. Moving through these thoughts and words were some of the hardest years of my life, but I would do it all over again to get to where I am today.

I no longer call my inner critic an "inner critic" because that name didn't do it justice. Today, my inner critic resembles a gremlin named *Absence.* My inner cheerleader also has a new name. When I used to imagine my inner cheerleader, I pictured red pompoms like from the movie *Bring It On,* which didn't do her justice either. Now, my inner cheerleader is a goddess warrior named *Athena.*

I urge you to do the same: name and draw your inner voices. This is an activity I do with my clients so they can take back power in who and what their identity looks and feels like. When you can visually see their entities, you can differentiate the voices and recognize who they are and what they are saying. For the inner critic, it helps to see that voice isn't as scary as what you hear in your head. For the inner cheerleader, it allows you to step into a voice and become who you want to be.

When I drew my gremlin for the first time, it looked evil with pointy ears, jagged teeth, thick mucus dripping from its mouth, long disheveled fingernails, and scales on its slightly hunched-over body. *Absence* can turn into mist and fog just like a scary movie, where that thick dark fog consumes you and you can't see a way out.

BRAIN TRAINING EXERCISE: INNER VOICE PORTRAYALS

1. **Draw it.** Use markers, crayons, or pencil. Bring your inner critic to life on a piece of paper. I want you to be able to see it right in front of you instead of what your imagination creates in your mind.
3. **Name it.** Give it a name that isn't a close family or friend. We want to depersonalize the inner critic so you can separate it from you.
4. **Voice it.** Pay attention to the tone of voice. Then, choose a voice you would use with a child or a pet, or that you hear as

comical. When your inner critic speaks to you now, I want you to use this new voice instead. By changing your inner critic's original voice, you take power away from it.

5. **Thank it.** On days your inner critic decides to make an appearance, I want you to visualize your drawing and the new voice. Then I want you to say, "Thank you, *Absence.* You have protected me and got me to where I am today, but I no longer need your help." It is crucial to be aware and thank your inner critic because it has gotten you to where you are today and kept you safe but it doesn't have to be the only voice you now hear.
6. Now do the same exercise with your inner cheerleader. Change cheerleader to something of your choosing. Draw her, name her, voice her, and thank her for being here with you now because her voice is the voice you want to hear.

The purpose of having an inner voice has two theories: to be able to use language to regulate our own behaviour and actions, and to help commit information and experiences to memory. Many researchers have called it different things: inner speech, self-talk, silent speech, verbal thinking, inner monologue, inner dialogue, inner voice, and voice imagery (because, yes, some people see pictures instead of words).[46] To me, both theories play a part in how the inner critic voice can diminish your confidence. My interpretation of how all of this fits together is this: if you have an experience and view it undesirably, your inner critic helps commit that experience to memory, thereby defining what future experiences will be like. This affects how you show up or how you stay stuck. Your inner voice, whether inner critic or inner cheerleader, plays a large part in your happiness, identity, and worth.

For example, if your inner critic tells you, *you can't do that,* and you make a mistake, there's more of a chance that you stop trying and commit to memory that *you're not good enough.*

How you choose to speak to yourself has a profound impact on your emotional, mental, spiritual, and physical well-being. You become your judge, jury, and verdict. Your happiness, your identity, your worth, and your darkness are all defined by you.

Your mind is rarely quiet and it's not supposed to be. Your mind is supposed to think, ponder, wonder, hope, and dream. When a thought presents itself, it is your interpretation of the thought that changes its meaning altogether. If you alter your thought, substitute to words you believe, you then get to change how you feel about you and about the journey you experience. Your inner voice is completely in your control.

CHAPTER 19

THE DUALITY OF DARKNESS

There is a darkness in each one of us that we have to learn how to navigate and mold to our interpretation. The darkness can soothe but the darkness can also swallow us whole. I've experienced both, but when I feel consumed by the darkness that swallows me whole, I have a hard time finding my way out. It feels as if I am being held underwater, thrashing for my life, my lungs trying to gasp for air, screaming in agony while my inner voice continues to hold me under and my mind is too scared to think or act. When I am in this place, there is no ending or beginning, it is only a void. Parts of my body feel pain and hurt while my mind feels numb and motionless. In this void, my inner gremlin lives and keeps me company, but that is not the company I am searching for or deserve.

A few years ago, I made a choice that I didn't want to remain in that void anymore. That was all it took. One choice forever changed my future: the choice to ask for help from my psychiatrist, my trust squad, and my inner goddess warrior. That first step allowed me to take the next step and then the next, eventually getting me to where I am today, living with and accepting my darkness for what it is: a place where I can be both safe and vulnerable. For the longest time I let my inner gremlin and my darkness define me, but it wasn't my entire being, just like it isn't your entire being either.

Darkness has long been viewed as a scary and frightening place, and even more so for women, who are taught to look over their shoulders when they walk alone at night. We are told at an early age to fear it, and even movies show us the dark is where monsters and creatures come out to play. But this narrative isn't completely accurate, because the dark is also where night comes to life. The stars and moon shine bright, and animals like owls, hares, and fireflies come alive. The dark can be what you choose to make it, if only you think differently. This is how I choose to view my darkness, and my inner goddess warrior gets to dance among the stars and feel the freeness of her power and strength. It has taken me years to change and alter my interpretation of my own darkness, and I continue to explore it so I can learn and grow as a human being and as a woman.

I started Part IV with a quote: "'There are different kinds of darkness,' Rhys said. I kept my eyes shut. 'There is the darkness that frightens, the darkness that soothes, the darkness that is restful.' I pictured each. 'There is the darkness of lovers, and the darkness of assassins. It becomes what the bearer wishes it to be, needs it to be. It is not wholly bad or good.'"

This quote describes the beauty that comes with darkness. It's recognizing that the darkness in each one of us is a part of us; this darkness also makes us whole. It is in the dark that there can be scary monsters, like the inner gremlin, but the same darkness is also the place where you can dream among the moon and stars, as well as thank your inner gremlin and acknowledge what you have learned. You can return to it because your inner goddess finds rest and peace while she slumbers. You get to choose how you view your darkness.

In Japanese culture, there is the art of kintsugi, which is mending broken pottery with gold. When I thought I was broken, those voids that opened became that deep, dark abyss, and I thought those voids, my stories, defined me for the worse. But that's because of how I chose to interpret it and how I chose to speak to myself about those stories. I now see the darkness differently. The darkness isn't a void; instead, it's a place I learned to put myself back together, piece by piece. Within that darkness, I mended myself with remnants of gold: my growth, my wisdom, and my inner goddess warrior. This book is the first time I have expressed how one can live with their darkness, and I hope you use this as an opportunity to explore and connect with both your darkness and your gold.

Francesca (whom I talked about in Part I) continued to work with me because she knew her inner gremlin had spent years tearing her down, and that it would take time to reframe and empower her inner goddess warrior. It was easy for Francesca to slip back into never feeling enough and blaming herself: *What if I did things differently? Maybe then they would like me and include me.* And if something went wrong, it was very natural that she followed it with *What did I do wrong?*

Over many months, I asked her to challenge that question, examine the environment, reset her expectation, and ask a different question. Reflecting and evaluating these situations takes practice and time, and I didn't expect Francesca to get it all on the first go, nor do I expect you to get it on the first go either. My suggestion to you as you navigate and start to alter your inner gremlin is to give yourself permission to be kind, compassionate, and gentle with yourself on this new adventure.

When Francesca and I first started working together, I could tell her workplace was a toxic environment. Undermining, lies, gossip, and belittling all took place, yet Francesca blamed herself, thinking if she was better, then they would like her and she would fit in. For those who are stuck in IP, perfectionism, and burnout, they can't accurately assess themselves and the environment.

In the early stages of COVID-19 we saw what society deemed "The Great Resignation," and as I'm writing this part of the book,

I am hearing rumbles of "The Great Regret." Let's explore this. The Great Resignation happened because employees saw their work environment for what it was, decided they'd had enough, and left. During this time, they found a new job or career, and with new changes came a honeymoon phase. However, if they didn't do the inner work of figuring out what their needs and wants were first, then it was easy to drift from one toxic work environment to another.

I believe that a lack of inner work navigating one's inner gremlin means they won't be able to distinguish between a toxic work environment or a healthy one, because the inner gremlin makes it easy to blame oneself. This is why people are now calling it "The Great Regret"; the honeymoon phase is over, and the inner gremlins still tell them they're not capable, that every job is shit, and that that's what they deserve.

If that's the case with you—if your inner gremlin is saying, *Well you should have stayed at that other shitty job because at least you knew what that shit was about*—it's not too late. It's actually never too late. At any point in time, you can make the decision that you've heard enough from your inner gremlin and you are now choosing to reframe your thoughts and activate your inner goddess warrior.

It would have been easy for me to outline why Francesca's environment wasn't working for her and push her into leaving and finding a new job, but that wouldn't help answer the questions *What did I do wrong?* and *Am I enough?* This is why I have put together my coaching program, so women can navigate and alter their inner critic and be confident in their decisions. That is how you get out of your comfort zone, out of being scared and into where you want and know you can be.

On one of our coaching calls, Francesca updated me about a new work opportunity. She was beyond enthralled. She never thought these opportunities would ever be possible. In that same breath, she told me about a shocking revelation. Her assistant would be leaving the current office as well because she recognized it was an environment she didn't want to be in either. During that conversation, Francesca's assistant said to her, "Well, now that I am leaving, I feel I should share something with you because I know I won't get in trouble anymore."

"What do you mean?" Francesca asked.

Her assistant informed her that the co-owners had pulled all the staff members aside, without Francesca, and let them know that they would be firing her in a few months. They told everyone to keep their mouths shut, and to not respect her while they waited the time out. Francesca was floored when she heard this. When she shared the information with me, I was stunned and speechless, and that doesn't happen too often. I asked Francesca to walk me through her thought process as she navigated this new information.

Francesca explained, "I don't feel devastated. It's not a surprise."

I replied, "What do you feel right now?"

She took a moment to think. "It actually feels like relief."

She paused again, "Buuutttt, my gremlin in my head is saying the owner saw my work and thought that it was terrible. But when that voice came up, I immediately opposed it with: 'But you *are* good enough.'"

I could hear the tone of her voice shift.

She continued. "In that moment, as I watched that inner voice change, I knew I am strong and brave."

I smiled from ear to ear. Francesca heard her inner gremlin but recognized it didn't have to be the only voice. I continued to ask Francesca questions to revisit why her inner gremlin was able to speak unkindly to her for so long. "Why do you think your work is terrible?"

She reminded herself that in the past, various people,

including her mom, an instructor, and now her boss, had all made snide comments during impressionable moments in her life that reinforced her inner gremlin. Yet, Francesca had evidence from herself that showed she was capable and skilled.

In past sessions, Francesca and I had altered her mantra *I need to be perfect* to *I am good enough.*

On this call, I challenged her to take it one step further. "What if we changed *I am good enough* to *I am good*?"

Both of us were silent, as Francesca pondered what I said.

Francesca replied, "What if I can't believe that?"

"What if you can't believe that . . . yet? I'm not saying you need to brag about everything you do. I'm not saying boast to the world that you are amazing and incredible. I'm not even saying you need to say you are great. All I am saying is you can remind yourself, *I am good.*'"

With lightness in Francesca's voice, she said, "I can definitely believe that."

I shared with Francesca my perspective of her over the past few months—how she had worked immensely to change her inner gremlin, how she had grown her capacity to be able to have these difficult conversations without walking away crying, completely devastated thinking she was unable to make changes. I showed her how she had started to develop her own leadership philosophy of how she wants to build a work culture and how she wants to lead, how she has the ability to reflect and process challenges without putting them off or thinking she can't handle them. And I reminded her how she has more opportunities now because she has stepped into a more confident self. I showed her that even though she can't believe in herself every minute of every day, she is slowly stepping into her confidence.

I ended the coaching call by reminding her how far she has come, which at times the high achiever forgets to reflect on. Let me remind you there is no way you are here today reading this book because you waited for something just to happen to you. You are more than lucky. You have already made the decision to be a high achiever. It's time you start believing in you.

When Francesca and I initially started working together, she never thought in a million years she would consider starting her own business. I am happy to say that as of today, Francesca's office is under construction, and she is well on her way to becoming the leader she now knows she can be.

CHAPTER 20

SCIENCE AND MAGIC

Neuroplasticity is the brain's ability to adapt, modify, and create new neural networks throughout life.[47] [48] Not only is it adjusting its connections but it's reorganizing the structure and function of the nervous system. Yup, that means you can reorganize your FF response and other circuitry. This brings me back to the mindset–bodyset connection and how changing your inner gremlin to inner goddess warrior has an impact confirmed by neuroscience.

I know what you're thinking: *Wooooaaaahhh, no way.* Yes way. Now, if science says so, what if there was a magical way of changing the way you think? There is. Say it with me: *Abracadabra.* The literal translation of *abracadabra* is "I will create as I speak."[49] This means if your inner goddess warrior chooses kinder words, it will change the way you feel, change how your body reacts, and change your confidence.

Let me clarify now that science and magic have come together, and there is still no magic pill. Changing your narrative to allow your inner goddess warrior to be the primary voice you hear takes time, practice, and patience. As you begin to separate your inner gremlin from who you are and what you want to be, your inner goddess warrior begins to lead the way. Think of it like hiking with a guide. Your inner gremlin has been your guide for some time now, and that hiking trail is well marked. There is a specific path you take each time where trees line the way. Your inner gremlin threw pebbles down, making that path easily walkable. It's comfortable and familiar.

This path is no longer what you need or want. A new path needs to be made, and to do that you need to grab new hiking shoes, hiking poles, and maybe even a machete to cut down some forest overgrowth. Each time you take this new path, the trail becomes clearer. Maybe you lay down new rocks and remove some trees. And you know who is on this trail with you? Your inner goddess warrior, who is supportive, kind, and caring. Eventually, the old inner gremlin trail doesn't appear familiar, and soon enough, overgrowth covers its tracks.

There will be a point in time when you have to actively and consciously make the decision to take the new path. It's hard, challenging, and downright dirty but it is worth it. You always have a choice at that fork in the road: choose the gremlin or choose the goddess warrior. If you choose the inner gremlin path, eventually that path will become paved and it will be harder to stop. If you choose the inner goddess warrior path, it will be challenging in the beginning. Some days you may even fall off the trail and cut yourself on a thorny rose bush, but your inner goddess warrior will be there to support you.

Creating this new trail is 100 percent possible, because what I just described is neuroplasticity at its finest. It is the brain's ability to create new neural networks throughout your entire life. Together we have explored the impostor cycle, the perfectionism cycle, and the anxiety cycle. Now, with neuroplasticity, you get to create a new cycle: *The Empowered Cycle.*

Let me take you through this new cycle. On the left side, you will see the initial thought awareness creating a different bodyset reaction, one that allows you to activate your inner goddess warrior. When she comes along, you set realistic expectations and sustainable work patterns. This leads to your success that you not only notice but absorb and believe!

Moving down on the diagram, by resetting to a realistic rulebook, you alter your thinking style, behaviours, and expectations.

Now you get to embrace the new evidence of success or practice self-compassion while reflecting.

Last, but definitely not least, when defining sustainable work patterns you get to schedule time blocks, implement boundaries, and control your time and energy while nurturing healthy habits and building resilience. You become a priority. All of this was made possible by choosing a new inner narrative: the one spoken by your inner goddess warrior.

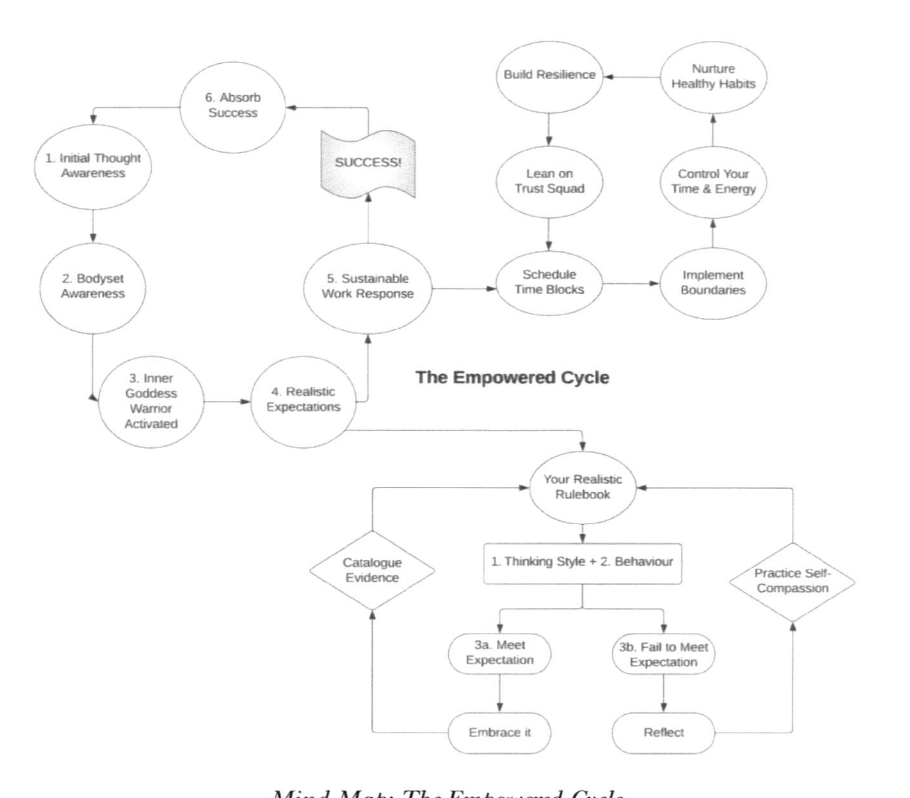

Mind Map: The Empowered Cycle

CHAPTER 21

FINAL THOUGHTS

Recently, I was involved in my first big financial deal with business partners. I can't go into specifics, however, what I can tell you is that even after healing and changing your inner gremlin, you may not be able to completely silence your inner gremlin altogether.

I woke up at four-thirty that morning in a panic. Today was the day before closing the deal, and we were finalizing paperwork. There were things on my to-do list. I was tired and had been tired for a couple of weeks. I had traveled and was still trying to catch up on my sleep. My sleep has always been a challenge, even during childhood when I had severe night terrors and nightmares. At times, I have to remind myself I'm safe before I go to bed so my FF response doesn't get activated. I don't watch scary movies or shows before bed, let alone action thrillers, because if I do I'll relive them at night in my dreams. I digress, but I wanted to set the stage of what happens after years of sleep deprivation. It's hard to function and navigate your thoughts, emotions, and FF response. This is why, in Part III, I stressed cultivating routines and figuring out your self-care needs.

At this point of the deal-closing day, I was awake but overtired, which came with heavy emotions. I launched myself to the computer, where I was unable to find a document I needed, and in that moment, my inner gremlin broke through its cage. All my old thoughts came rushing back. *You're such a failure. You're letting people down.*

I condemned myself over and over as I searched for that document. My inner gremlin knew where to poke further at me, *You can't coach others if you can't even figure out your own shit.* This was a brutal reminder that old voices die hard and live in the depths of one's darkness. That gremlin once used to be the only voice I heard, and now I was shocked I heard it at all. As my gremlin stood there, leaning with one hand on its hip and nonchalantly examining its nails, it sneered, *I told you. I told you you'd never be good enough.*

I stared right at it for what felt like hours but was only a few minutes, and I realized the trickster had tried to trap my inner goddess warrior in its cage. But she ran with all her might out of those depths of darkness like a warrior getting ready for battle. She took her stance and stood in front of my inner gremlin. On alert, she surveyed the environment, lowered her weapons, and told my gremlin, *Thank you, but no, I have it from here.*

My inner gremlin turned its back to me and sauntered toward its cage. It stopped at one point, looked over its shoulder with a smirk only Loki, the god of mischief, would give, and closed its cage door. It knew its place. They had both battled it out for years but the war was officially over. As I heard the cage door click shut, way down in the depths of my darkness, my FF response settled, my heart stopped thudding, tears went away, my mind became clearer, and I knew what I needed to do. I took a couple of long breaths and got to work.

Old voices die hard and live deep in our darkness. That inner gremlin never goes away because it is a part of us. For me, I've created a cage for my inner gremlin because it allows me to separate it from who I am, who I want to be, and what I know I am worthy of.

Both your gremlin and warrior goddess can exist inside you; however, you get to choose which voice speaks to you. You choose your tone, pitch and volume. *You* choose *your* words. And if you wouldn't say it to a loved one or friend, then why would you think it's okay to say to you?

Speak kindly, you're listening.

ME AND I

You and I, played our parts
You and I, gave our hearts
You and I, it was no doubt
You and I, figured it out
You and I, balance undone
You and I, no arguments won
You and I, regrets were made
You and I, time went unpaid
You and I, underestimated worth
You and I, too far from earth
You and I, broke and torn
But Me and I, again reborn

— Dr. Jessica E. Metcalfe

ACKNOWLEDGEMENTS

First and foremost, I want to thank myself. Seriously, you just read a book on how to savour success and own your inner goddess warrior, so I'm doing that right now. Thank you, Athena, for taking me on this journey because it has been a thrilling ride, and I am looking forward to all the future possibilities, especially The Speak Kindly Experience which includes more books.

To my trust squad members, Keely and Alero: I don't think I would have stepped away from the years of isolation due to COVID-19 and into the headspace and heart space I was in if it wasn't for both of you. You held my puzzle pieces when I couldn't hold them on my own. Through the many tears, shock, awe, and giggles, you are the family I get to choose.

To my cancer patients, thank you for everything you taught me: that success and happiness aren't on the opposite side of retirement, because not everyone makes it. Thank you for trusting in me to be the dentist I knew how to be.

To my family by blood: we have faced challenges together and will continue to face them, but I wouldn't trade it for the world.

To my editor, Hannah Rumsey: HOLY SHIT, I DID IT! Thank you for all of the joy you brought into my life through the writing and editing process. One of the first things you said to me was, "Don't look at the red comments as if I'm grading you and it is wrong. These are me asking more questions to make sure you get the story across that you want." Thank you for fist-pumping the air with me every time our Zoom calls started, and thank you for answering my emails when my own inner gremlin reared its head.

And to my readers: Thank you for coming along for the ride and adventure. Who knew it would be so bumpy yet thrilling? You are amazing, wonderful and awesome. Don't you ever forget it.

ENDNOTES

[1] Clance, P. R., & Imes, S. A. (1978). The imposter phenomenon in high achieving women: Dynamics and therapeutic intervention. Psychotherapy, 15(3), 241–247. doi: https://doi.org/10.1037/h0086006

[2] Sakulku, J. (2011). The Impostor Phenomenon. *The International Journal of Behavioral Science, 6*(1), 75–97. doi: https://doi.org/10.14456/ijbs.2011.6

[3] Neureiter, M., & Traut-Mattausch, E. (2016). An Inner Barrier to Career Development: Preconditions of the Impostor Phenomenon and Consequences for Career Development. Frontiers in Psychology, 7. Retrieved from https://www.frontiersin.org/article/10.3389/fpsyg.2016.00048

[4] Personal Care Products Council. (2020). *Our Economic & Social Impact.* Retrieved from https://www.personalcarecouncil.org/about-us/economic-impact-study/

[5] Hibberd, J. (2019). The imposter cure: How to stop feeling like a fraud and escape the mind-trap of imposter syndrome. Hachette UK.

[6] Scott, M., Yeung, H. H., Gick, B., & Werker, J. F. (2013). Inner speech captures the perception of external speech. The Journal of the Acoustical Society of America, 133(4), EL286–EL292. doi: https://doi.org/10.1121/1.4794932

[7] Scott, M., Yeung, H. H., Gick, B., & Werker, J. F. (2013). Inner speech captures the perception of external speech. The Journal of the Acoustical Society of America, 133(4), EL286–EL292. doi: https://doi.org/10.1121/1.4794932

[8] Robichaud, M., & Buhr, K. (2018). The worry workbook: CBT skills to overcome worry and anxiety by facing the fear of uncertainty. New Harbinger Publications, Inc.

[9] Young, V. (2011). *The secret thoughts of successful women: Why capable people suffer from the impostor syndrome and how to thrive in spite of it.* Crown Business.

[10] Van der Kolk, B. A. (2015). *The body keeps the score: Brain, mind, and body in the healing of trauma.* New York, New York: Penguin Books.

[11] Connell, S. (2022). *The Science of Getting Rich for Women: Your Secret Path to Millions.* Muse Literary.

[12] Mark, G., Iqbal, S., Czerwinski, M., & Johns, P. (2015). Focused, Aroused, but so Distractible: Temporal Perspectives on Multitasking and Communications. In *Proceedings of the 18th ACM Conference on Computer Supported Cooperative Work & Social Computing,* 903–916. doi: https://doi.org/10.1145/2675133.2675221

[13] Achor, S. (2010). *The happiness advantage: How a positive brain fuels success in work and life.* Crown Business.

[14] Zwicky, A. (2005, August 7). *Just Between Dr. Language and I* [blog post]. Retrieved from http://itre.cis.upenn.edu/~myl/languagelog/archives/002386.html

[15] Tewfik, B. A. (2021). The Impostor Phenomenon Revisited: Examining the Relationship Between Workplace Impostor Thoughts and Interpersonal Effectiveness at Work. Academy of Management Journal. doi: https://doi.org/10.5465/amj.2020.1627

[16] Tewfik, B. A. (2021). The Impostor Phenomenon Revisited: Examining the Relationship Between Workplace Impostor Thoughts and Interpersonal Effectiveness at Work. Academy of Management Journal. doi: https://doi.org/10.5465/amj.2020.1627

[17] Harari, D., Swider, B. W., Steed, L. B., & Breidenthal, A. P. (2018). Is Perfect Good? A Meta-analysis of Perfectionism in the Workplace. Journal of Applied Psychology, 103(10), 1121–1144. doi: https://doi.org/10.1037/apl0000324

[18] Ibid.
[19] Ibid.
[20] Brown, B. (2010). *The gifts of imperfection: Let go of who you think you're supposed to be and embrace who you are.* Hazelden.
[21] Frost, R. O., Marten, P., Lahart, C., & Rosenblate, R. (1990). The dimensions of perfectionism. Cognitive Therapy and Research, 14(5), 449–468. doi:10.1007/BF01172967
[22] Beck, A. T. (1979). *Cognitive therapy and the emotional disorders.* Penguin Group.
[23] Dozois, D. J. A., & Beck, A. T. (2008). Chapter 6 - Cognitive Schemas, Beliefs and Assumptions. In K. S. Dobson, & D. J. A. Dozois (Eds.), *Risk factors in depression* (pp. 119–143). San Diego: Elsevier. doi: https://doi.org/10.1016/B978-0-08-045078-0.00006-X
[24] Ackerman, C.E. (2017, September 29). *Cognitive Distortions: 22 Examples & Worksheets (& PDF).* PositivePsychology.com. Retrieved from https://positivepsychology.com/cognitive-distortions/
[25] Centre for Clinical Interventions. (2019, October 24). *Looking After Yourself: Perfectionism* [online modules]. Retrieved from https://www.cci.health.wa.gov.au/Resources/Looking-After-Yourself/Perfectionism
[26] Robichaud, M., & Buhr, K. (2018). *The worry workbook: CBT skills to overcome worry and anxiety by facing the fear of uncertainty.* New Harbinger Publications, Inc.
[27] Ibid.
[28] Maslach, C. (1982). *Burnout: The cost of caring.* Cambridge, MA: Malor Books.
[29] World Health Organization. (2019, May 8). Burn-out an "occupational phenomenon"*: International Classification of Diseases.* Retrieved from https://www.who.int/news/item/28-05-2019-burn-out-an-occupational-phenomenon-international-classification-of-diseases

[30] Henning, K., Ey, S., & Shaw, D. (1998). Perfectionism, the impostor phenomenon and psychological adjustment in medical, dental, nursing and pharmacy students. Medical Education, 32(5), 456–464. doi: https://doi.org/10.1046/j.1365-2923.1998.00234.x

[31] Bravata, D. M., Watts, S. A., Keefer, A. L., Madhusudhan, D. K., Taylor, K. T., Clark, D. M., . . . Hagg, H. K. (2020). Prevalence, Predictors, and Treatment of Impostor Syndrome: A Systematic Review. Journal of General Internal Medicine, 35(4), 1252–1275. doi: https://doi.org/10.1007/s11606-019-05364-1%20

[32] Leung, L. (2006). *Using perfectionism, imposter phenomenon and occupational field to predict job burnout.* California State University, Long Beach.

[33] LaDonna, K., Ginsburg, S. & Watling, C. (2018). "Rising to the level of your incompetence": What physicians' self-assessment of their performance reveals about the imposter syndrome in medicine. *Academic Medicine, 93*(5), 763–768. doi:10.1097/ACM.0000000000002046

[34] Achor, S. (2010). *The happiness advantage: How a positive brain fuels success in work and life.* Crown Business.

[35] Butler, G., & Mathews, A. (1987). Anticipatory anxiety and risk perception. Cognitive therapy and research, 11(5), 551–565. doi: https://doi.org/10.1007/BF01183858 American Psychological Association, APA PsycNet psycnet.apa.org/record/1988-10685-001

[36] Fletcher, J., & Stott, D. (2021). *Untangle your anxiety: a guide to overcoming an anxiety disorder by two people who have been through it.* Self-published.

[37] Bernier, D. (1998). A study of coping: Successful recovery from severe burnout and other reactions to severe work-related stress. Work & Stress, 12(1), 50–65. doi:10.1080/02678379808256848 American Psychological Association, APA PsycNet psycnet.apa.org/record/1998-10624-005

[38] van Dam, A. (2021). A clinical perspective on burnout: Diagnosis, classification, and treatment of clinical burnout. European Journal of Work and Organizational Psychology, 30(5), 732–741. doi:10.1080/1359432X.2021.1948400

[39] Tawwab, N. G. (2021). *Set boundaries, find peace: A guide to reclaiming yourself.* TarcherPerigee.

[40] Oxford Reference. (2022). *Overview: empathy.* Retrieved from https://www.oxfordreference.com/view/10.1093/oi/authority.20110803095750102

[41] American Psychological Association. (2020, February 1). Building your resilience. Retrieved from https://www.apa.org/topics/resilience/building-your-resilience

[42] American Psychological Association. (2022, May). Resilience. Retrieved from https://www.apa.org/topics/resilience

[43] Pignatiello, G. A., Martin, R. J., & Hickman, R. L. (2020). Decision fatigue: A conceptual analysis. *Journal of Health Psychology, 25*(1), 123–135. doi: https://doi.org/10.1177/1359105318763510

[44] Brown, B. (2021). *Atlas of the heart: Mapping meaningful connection and the language of human experience.* Random House.

[45] Holt-Lunstad, J., Smith, T. B., & Layton, J. B. (2010). Social Relationships and Mortality Risk: A Meta-analytic Review. PLOS Medicine, 7(7), e1000316. doi:10.1371/journal.pmed.1000316

[46] Alderson-Day, B., & Fernyhough, C. (2015). Inner speech: Development, cognitive functions, phenomenology, and neurobiology. Psychological Bulletin, 141(5), 931–965. doi:10.1037/bul0000021 National Library of Medicine, https://pubmed.ncbi.nlm.nih.gov/26011789/

[47] Cramer, S. C., Sur, M., Dobkin, B. H., O'Brien, C., Sanger, T. D., Trojanowski, J. Q., . . . Vinogradov, S. (2011). Harnessing neuroplasticity for clinical applications. Brain, 134(6), 1591–1609. doi:10.1093/brain/awr039

[48] Reeve, J. (2018). *Understanding motivation and emotion.* John Wiley & Sons.
[49] Kushner, L. (1993). *The book of words: Talking spiritual life, living spiritual talk.* Jewish Lights Publishing.

Made in United States
Troutdale, OR
04/23/2024